THOSE WHO HAVE KNOWN CLOSE ENCOUNTERS

UFO contactees often speak of an impending New Age wherein humankind will attain a new consciousness, a new awareness, and a higher state—or frequency—of vibration.

The UFO intelligences, they say, come from higher dimensions all around us which function on different vibratory levels, just as there are various radio frequencies....

As I state repeatedly in this book, someone has been broadcasting certain essential universal truths ever since man became man. Certain human receptors—that is, prophets and revelators—have been tuning in to those cosmic frequencies for centuries, because they, for some indeterminate reason, have been able to receive the channels with greater clarity than their more distracted or disinterested brethren.

Brad Steiger

THE
FELLOWSHIP

Spiritual Contact Between Humans and Outer Space Beings

Brad Steiger

IVY BOOKS • NEW YORK

This book is for Sherry, who helped me pick up the pieces and reassemble them, and helped me edit this book; for Hope, who never lost faith and never stopped working; and for Kermit, who has known of the "Fellowship" for many, many years.

Contents

God is in his heavens, all is wrong with the world. Man needs a god much closer to home, a god within himself. If God is not there, life is an outrageous terror ruled by Fate, which has no answers, only appointments. Nobody can live with Death before his eyes and the knowledge of the nothingness of all things. Life must have a meaning . . .

—INGMAR BERGMAN

I

Our Fellowship with Space Intelligences

UFO contactees are men and women who claim to receive messages, advice, or instruction from the occupants of spaceships, or flying saucers. I have been studying such men and women since 1967. With their emphasis upon spiritual teachings being transmitted to Earth by Space Beings, these UFO prophets have not only brought God physically to this planet, but they have created a blend of science and religion that offers a theology more applicable to modern humankind.

"Life must have a meaning," the philosophical among us have pleaded for centuries. If, as contact with extraterrestrial or other-dimensional intelligences would seem to suggest, we are not alone in the universe, then life does have a meaning, for we become part of a larger community of intelligences. We become evolving members in a hierarchy of cosmic citizenship.

Dr. Gordon Melton, Director of the Institute of the Study of American Religion, has commented that the UFO contactees are best understood as "an emerging religious movement with an impetus and a life of their own."

The UFO contactees may be evolving prototypes of a future evangelism. They may be the heralds of a New Age religion, a blending of technology and traditional religious concepts.

To many people, the very notion of an extraterrestrial or multidimensional entity contacting an Earthling belongs to the speculations of science fiction writers. Even the majority of researchers who specialize in the study of UFOs seem almost categorically to deny accounts of contact between *Homo sapiens* and alien species. However, reports of occupants sighted near landed UFOs have been carefully analyzed and, in certain dramatic instances, thoroughly documented.

It was the late Dr. J. Allen Hynek, the astronomer who for more than twenty years served as a consultant to the U.S. Air Force on its Project Blue Book Study of UFOs, who coined the term "close encounter of the third kind" to classify an interaction between a citizen of Earth and the humanoid occupant of a UFO. In 1976, Dr. Hynek told author Timothy Green Beckley that the Center for UFO Studies had an estimated 800 such reports on file.

There are several theories as to the UFOnauts' actual place of origin and their true identity. Every investigator, regardless of how open-minded he may hope to be, has his favorite location, whether physical or ethereal, for the agents of the apparently universal and timeless UFO phenomenon. Generally, these arguments are distilled to the central issue of whether the UFO intelligences are essentially nonphysical entities from an invisible realm in our own world, or physical beings who have the ability to attain a state of invisibility and to materialize and dematerialize both their bodies and their vehicles.

Perhaps both theories are correct. We may be con-

fronted by both kinds of intelligence in our spiritual, intellectual, biological, and evolutionary process.

Or we may be dealing with an intelligence that has a
physical structure so totally unlike ours that it presents
itself in a variety of guises, and employs invisibility,
materialization, and dematerialization at different times in
order to accomplish its goal of communication with our
species.

UFO contactees often speak of an impending New Age
wherein humankind will attain a new consciousness, a new
awareness, and a higher state—or frequency—of vibration.
They speak of each physical body being in a state of
vibration and of all things vibrating at their individual
frequencies.

The UFO intelligences, they say, come from higher
dimensions all around us which function on different vibratory levels, just as there are various radio frequencies
operating simultaneously in our environment. We can attune ourselves to these higher dimensions in much the
same manner as a radio receiver tunes in to the frequencies
of broadcasting stations. Different entities travel on various frequencies, according to their vibratory rate.

Then the question arises whether such information comes
from the contactee's own higher self or from a separate
and distinct outside intelligence. Certain investigators, whose
search for the truth about UFO contact will simply not
permit them to accept the validity of channelled messages,
must wonder if such entities as spirit guides, angels, or
Space Beings might be but externalized projections of the
contactee's own personality.

Parapsychologists have generally agreed that the *polter-
geist*, the "noisy ghost" that levitates objects and generally raises havoc in a household, is not an autonomous
being at all, but the externalized aggression of someone
undergoing the emotional stress of a severe adjustment
problem. Psychology maintains the axiom that whatever

the conscious mind represses, the unconscious embodies in allegorical form, either in dreams or in conscious creative imagery. Demons, for example, often serve as personifications of undesirable emotions, such as lust and hatred.

Angels and Space Beings could be the externalization of religious feelings that have been progressively denied expression in an increasingly secular world. The fact that the Space Beings' contacts seem definitely to be accelerating around the world could constitute a serious affirmation of man's need to fashion a new religious structure that will satisfy the basic spiritual requirements of the psyche while, at the same time, presenting an intelligent adaptation to space-age society.

Voices from Space

In the fall of 1956 one of the engineers at a major electronics firm in Cedar Rapids, Iowa, called a friend of mine and asked if he might bring a tape to his home that had been recorded the evening before.

"It appears that they were having their scanning device going to see if they could pick up any signals from outer space," my friend recalled for me. "While they were tuned in, a voice started talking that appeared to be emanating from an indeterminate point thousands of miles from Earth. As I understood the engineer, it would have been impossible for this voice to have come from this planet, but it had talked on for nearly two hours.

"I listened to the tape for at least thirty minutes. The voice appeared to be sexless. It sounded almost mechanical. The material it was relaying was good, very worthwhile, but I did not recognize the source for any of it. From time to time it sounded like something one would expect to find in the *Upanishads*. At other times it seemed like a cross between Kahlil Gibran and the *Bhagavad-Gita*

. . . what one might term universal truths, free of any one particular Earth philosophy.

"A few nights later I once again received a call from the electronics firm. The engineer told me the voice was back and said that I should look at approximately two o'clock in the north sky. I have a pair of night binoculars which brings up the stars and moon very well. I went out and looked up, and there was an object moving perfectly horizontally from east to west across the sky. It appeared to be about one-third the size of the moon.

"It would move across the horizon, stop, remain stationary for a bit, then drop down a little lower, back up rapidly, and move once again across the horizon. It reminded me of a kind of cosmic typewriter moving across the sky, returning the carriage, dropping down a line, and typing another sentence. . . . It repeated this back-and-forth process six times before it accelerated speed terrifically fast and moved out of sight.

"The next morning the radio and papers said that the night before an erratic meteor had caused thousands of telephone problems. The Cedar Rapids electronics firm had a track on it, and so did stations in Omaha and Davenport. Apparently, as far as they were able to determine, the erratic 'meteor' was about three thousand miles distant from Earth. What they did not publish, of course, was that the erratic meteor was also a talking, metaphysical meteor."

Just as Arthur C. Clarke, in *2001: A Space Odyssey*, postulated mental beings from Jupiter who assumed a bit more than an academic interest in the cultural development of Earth's man-apes, perhaps we might conjecture soul beings from other dimensions who assumed an interest in humankind's spiritual development. When the Old Testament speaks of the *Elohim* creating people in their image, we might speculate that these Higher Intelligences were really more concerned with presenting humanity with a spiritual, rather than a physical, pattern for development. Whereas Clarke imagined his interplanetary tutors planting monoliths to probe the man-apes' minds, map their bodies, study their reactions, and evaluate their potentials so that they might one day evolve to explore the stars, we might imagine cosmic missionaries seeing to the implantation of spiritual truths in "human monoliths" so that humans might one day evolve to a New Age, spiritually equipped to explore new dimensions, new frequencies of being.

As I state repeatedly in this book, *someone* has been broadcasting certain essential universal truths ever since man became man. Certain human receptors—that is, prophets and revelators—have been tuning in to these cosmic frequencies for centuries, because they, for some indeterminate reason, have been able to receive the channels with greater clarity than their more distracted or disinterested brethren.

Revelations for Our Time

Dr. Walter Houston Clark, Professor Emeritus of Andover Theological Seminary, told me that the kind of revelation experience that has impressed him in recent years has been that which has sprung from greatly deepened religious sensitivity of a mystical nature. In Dr. Clark's opinion, such a sensitivity often leads to a greatly lessened valuation on external and material values in exchange for a strengthened valuation of the nonrational, and a heightened compassion with greater concern for others and for nature.

"On the basis of the knowledge of, and respect for, the mystical consciousness, which has been growing on me now for fifty years," Dr. Clark said, "I fully agree with William James' statement in his *Varieties of Religious Experience* to the effect that personal religion has its origin in the mystical consciousness. Succinctly, James expressed my position for me when he wrote in a letter to a friend: 'The mother sea and fountainhead of all religions lie in the mystical experience of the individual, taking the word mystical in a very wide sense. All theologies and all ecclesiasticisms are secondary growths superimposed.'

"I believe that all people are potential mystics, just as each one of us is a potential poet, artist, or ecstatic," Dr. Clark continued. "This hunger for the expression of the nonrational is sleeping within all of us. It goes beyond those valid needs of food, clothing, and shelter that keep our bodies alive. Nonrational and intangible values keep us alive by giving meaning to life, and whether consciously or unconsciously and though suppressed by the priority of material needs in our society, a sensitivity to them always has the possibility of being awakened by the proper stimuli. The longer this sensitivity is neglected or starved, the more spontaneous and forcefully it is expressed when it surfaces."

At this point in our research, it is impossible to offer a universally acceptable answer to the question of the true identity of the Space Beings who are allegedly communicating with the UFO mystics.

They may be God's angels coming to gather the elect in the Chariots of the Lord. They may be speaking to the UFO prophets in order to guide humankind through the difficult period of adjustment as the old, corrupt Piscean Age presents a transitional time of cleansing and purification before we enter the Age of Aquarius.

They may be our cosmic cousins, aliens from another world or dimension who, over the ages, have interacted with us in a very complex kind of symbiotic relationship, and who do not wish us to destroy the biosphere which is somehow very important to them, as well as to us.

Or maybe the contactees are only employing puppetlike projections of their own fantasies to voice the protest which humankind's collective unconscious may be screaming as it recoils from the hideous, scalding specter of nuclear annihilation, the unfathomable ecological truth of what may be the death of our biosphere by the poisonous fouling of our own nest, and the trauma of an old world dying and a new world being born.

Whoever or whatever the Space Beings may be—whether cosmic missionaries or projections of the Higher Self—the channelled material contained in this book may be the scriptures and theological treatises of the New Age.

As Dr. R. Leo Sprinkle, Director of Counseling and Testing and Associate Professor of Psychology at the University of Wyoming, has observed, "The UFO phenomenon is an important factor in the total experience of a new age, the merger of 'science' and 'religion.' "

Dr. Sprinkle has made an extensive study of the contactee experience and has listened to messages which suggest that there will be many changes in the condition of both Earth and humankind in the next twenty-five years. The contactees speak of catastrophic events, the likelihood of a future devastating World War, and a specific outcome in the struggle between the forces of "darkness" and of "light."

"I believe," Dr. Sprinkle concludes, "that we are confronted with a most exciting and most challenging task: to understand the physical, biological, psychosocial, and spiritual implications of the ending of a former age and the awakening of the 'New Age.' "

Ever since Dan Fry claimed to have been taken aboard a UFO for a rapid flight from the White Sands proving grounds in New Mexico to New York in the early 1950s, the engaging and articulate engineer has been kept busy on the flying-saucer lecture circuit. Once he spoke on the matter of the Space Beings' missionary zeal:

"We do have people on Earth who do similarly. We have men and women who go to undeveloped cultures. They don't do it to get fortune and fame. They do it because they feel they might be able to pass on some parts of our civilization to these people. They feel that they have something which might be useful or helpful or accepted by the primitive people they visit. We call them missionaries.

"The Space Brothers hope that we might take a little advice and avoid the approaching cataclysms, so that we might be able to continue as a species in the future. And just as some of our earthly missionaries have ended up in the stewpots of the primitive people they hoped to help, so have certain of the space travellers met equally ignominious fates at the hands of Earthlings. But from time to time, these cosmic missionaries descend to Earth to see if they can help keep us from destroying ourselves and our planet."

2

The Mystery of Semjase

D r. Fred Bell of Laguna Beach, California, claims that he is having a love affair with a woman from outer space.

If Dr. Bell's story is true, then he has experienced what may be the singularly most exciting, most important event of modern times. If he truly has established contact with a citizen from another world, then he has provided us with the only newsstory that can compete for planetary impact with the Return of Christ, the Rising of Atlantis, or the Formula for Eternal Youth and Health.

If he doesn't convince us that his friend is from another world, his love story may provoke us to think and to wonder. It may even inspire us and bring about a certain inner awareness that we did not previously recognize.

Most of the over one hundred books that I have written have concerned themselves with what I term "phenomenology," documented accounts of apparently strange, mysterious, inexplicable phenomena which are remarkable byproducts of humankind's interaction with its environment and its universe.

Why, after nearly twenty years of examining UFO contactees, would I place any emphasis and/or credence on Fred Bell's claims?

Because he has ostensibly received a lot of physical and scientific information, as opposed to the more or less standard contactee material of spiritually oriented cosmic sermonettes. Regardless of whether Dr. Bell's inspiration for various inventions designed to improve our health and our productivity originated in his creative Higher Self or in dialogue with an entity from "out there," the actual physical artifacts seem to have practical value to our society and its multitude of problems. If Bell can provide us with even a few solutions to the nightmarish problems of pollution, disease, and ineffective utilization of our resources, then we should give him a fair hearing.

I must admit to a certain knee-jerk reaction when I learned that Bell claimed to be in communication with an entity called Semjase. This particular UFOnaut, described as a beautiful, goddess-like blonde, is also the Starwoman in question in the controversial Billy Meier contactee case.

I am familiar with the investigators who believe this well-known Swiss "close encounter of the third kind" to be authentic and Meier's amazing photographs of spaceships to be genuine. I am also quite aware of the arguments of those investigators who believe most of the photographs to be hoaxed and who regard Meier with extreme suspicion. There are also those researchers who are willing to grant that Meier may have experienced an actual contact, but they suggest that he unwisely sought to offer physical "proof" to a doubting world by faking some colorful UFO photographs.

As a researcher, I am cautious in regard to contactee claims, but I remain open to the possibility that such people as Billy Meier and Fred Bell may each have a piece of a great cosmic jigsaw puzzle. I have come to the conclusion that some kind of external intelligence has interacted with humankind throughout history in an effort to learn more about us—or in an effort to communicate certain basic truths and concepts to our species. There is a subtle kind of symbiotic relationship which exists between humankind and UFO intelligences. They need us as much as we need them.

Since 1967, I have traveled throughout nearly all of the United States, a good deal of the Canadian provinces, and Puerto Rico to listen to the experiences of those men and women who claim extraterrestrial contact. It seemed only proper that I make the relatively short jump from Phoenix to Laguna Beach to meet Fred Bell.

His attractive multilevel home reflects the varied interests of the man. When I first entered his home ("Please take off your shoes"), I felt that I might have stumbled into the laboratory of the eccentric inventor in the film *Back to the Future*. But that was only on the first level.

On the next, I felt that the silent testimony of the keyboards and other musical instruments betrayed the home of a musician—though the chiropractor's adjustment table added a bizarre note to the arrangement. The third floor indicated the residence of an artist, a stereo buff, an astronomy enthusiast, and a photographer. At the same time, there were a number of devices that made it appear as though future science had been peeled off the covers of some old *Amazing Stories* pulp magazines and scattered about the room.

In addition to being a contactee, Fred Bell is a Renaissance Man. He is an inventor, a musician, an artist, a poet, an authority and lecturer on holistic health—and God knows what else. He is also a man who is very easy to talk with and who speaks very freely, frankly, and fluently about any topic you might care to place into the traffic pattern of conversation.

Bell is very much a student of energies and their practical applications to Earth's troubles and torments. His receptor disc, worn as a medallion, seems to be an essential element of his wardrobe. I have observed it worn over his turtleneck, as well as over his tuxedo. It is, according to Bell, a device that utilizes subtle energies that are all around us, assists in digestion, aids in the proper assimilation of food substances, and brings about a general sense of well-being.

Bell also believes strongly in "pyramid power." I know from reliable sources—and from a number of photographs—that he used to wear a small pyramid on his head at all times without any noticeable signs of embarrassment. When he makes a commitment to a philosophy or a point of view, it is obvious that Bell is not easily swayed from his conviction.

After a brief period of social amenities, I got right at the question of Bell's girlfriend from the Pleiades, that bright cluster of stars in the constellation Taurus. Classically referred to as the "Seven Sisters," the Pleiades are commonly mentioned in UFO lore as the home area of our stellar visitors.

Bell's first impression of Semjase was in 1971. It came to him as a telepathic image that kept repeating itself. Together with his roommate at the time, a guitar player, Fred began to sketch portraits in an attempt to capture the image that he was perceiving mentally. Then a lady friend, while doing a self-portrait, drew upon the energy that they were creating and perfected a rather accurate likeness of the beautiful Semjase.

From the beginning, Fred knew that the image of Semjase was familiar to him. He was convinced that he recognized her from a prior life experience on another planet and from a past existence on Earth, when he was an archaeologist who discovered evidence that the Pleiadeans had interacted with our planet's evolution.

"But Semjase would not give me her name at first," Fred told me. "Even after the physical contacts began. Semjase looks like she is about twenty-six or twenty-seven. The average lifespan for the Pleiadeans would probably be about nine hundred of our years."

For decades now, our scientists have speculated that if intelligent life existed elsewhere in the universe, the Pleiades would be one of the more likely candidates.

Semjase and her fellow crew members call their home planet "Erra." Bell, assuming a slightly professorial tone, told me that the Pleiadeans live in perfect harmony. "We have all kinds of things on Earth that create stress and really accelerate our aging processes which they have totally eliminated on Erra. If we could live in harmony with our own nature, we too could live for hundreds of years."

The buildings on Erra are circular, each with a certain amount of land around it. Horticulture is extremely popular among the Pleiadeans.

The inhabitants of Erra love to cultivate the land and to work with plants. They consider it one way to be close to nature and, therefore, close to God.

Bell agrees with the Pleiadeans' choice of circular rooms. "We conducted experiments and found that the worst-shaped room you can be inside of is a rectangular or square one. In such rooms, all forms of natural energy are broken into very disharmonious wave forms which affect the human aura in very negative ways."

The career-oriented on Erra undergo a minimum of seventy years of education.

"Even in my own ignorant way of being a cosmic student," Bell said, "I've been going to different kinds of schools for about thirty-five years now; and I'm just starting to realize that there's a whole lot more out there. There are orders of great, great magnitude. By comparison, I haven't finished nursery school yet!

"On Erra each citizen has an obligation to society which

is overseen by the High Council. Once a Pleiadean has completed his seventy years of basic schooling, he or she goes on into whatever career field is appropriate. In Semjase's case, she's one of those who goes around to different civilizations to act as a 'communicator.' And she's very good at it.''

On February 29, 1980, Bell received the following communication regarding pyramid energies from Semjase:

"Pyramid energies balance the human body when it is under stress. Those who utilize pyramid energies will be better able to survive the dramatic Earth changes that began in 1958 and will continue to the year 1998.

"Skeptics will become victims of the shifting of Earth's energy fields and will suffer great pain. They will be subject to the loss of their physical forms; and in their astral bodies, they will bear witness to the changing of the ages. Those who follow the precepts of pyramid energy will guide the remaining world through the Earth changes and will not suffer loss of physical form.''

Divine intervention had occurred on a more dramatic level on the ''conscious planes'' during the year 1980, as a ''messianic'' energy began to stimulate more people to an awareness of the presence of their ''brothers and sisters from the Pleiades.'' Lost souls from the astral plane would slowly begin reincarnating on Earth after the year 2001. The communication continued as follows:

"At the present time, Earth, Venus, and Jupiter are in an esoteric trine which will allow the birth of Christ Conscious souls to the physical plane. After 2001, Venus will shift; Mercury will take the place of Venus; and we will have a trine of Earth, Mercury, and Jupiter.

"At that time, we will witness the incarnation of the Super Souls, entities with advanced physical powers. These people will have the ability to work off higher Karma and to assist the souls of those men and women who lost their physical forms during the time of Earth changes and planetary adjustment. Those confused souls by that time have gained an appreciation of the divine attributes of form and will have begun to work off lower Karma so that an ascent might be accomplished to the Higher Realms.''

I asked Fred about the ''Super Souls'' that would be incarnating on Earth after the year 2001.

He explained that a ''Super Soul'' in the Pleiadean consciousness is comprised of the aggregate of several powerful soul essences. There is an evolved state of being between incarnations to which all these Super Souls go. At this level of evolution, they are all a part of the Super Soul of the Universe. After the year 2001, we will see an increased number of these highly evolved beings incarnating on Earth.

I pointed out to Fred that a great deal of research that I had conducted indicated that certain ''visitations'' to spaceships were out-of-body projections, rather than actual physical experiences.

Always courteous and—I am certain from *his* perspective—patient, Bell responded that he was familiar with out-of-body experiences (OBEs) and with astral projections. He shared an account of the time when, as a teenager, he had somehow managed to ''visit'' a girlfriend in Buffalo, New York, while he lay in the ''twilight zone'' between waking and sleeping in Stewartsville, Missouri.

''It wasn't like a dream at all,'' Fred recalled. ''It was like I was totally wide awake. In fact, I was a little worried about how I was going to get back to Stewartsville!''

Certain of his encounters with Semjase might somehow be related to astral trips, Bell conceded, but they are so much more physical in texture.

In 1971, years before Semjase as a known entity had become part of his life, Fred had undergone a remarkable physical projection. He had been aware of his physical body as he began to awaken in a spaceship. He was lying down with his head in the lap of a beautiful blonde woman.

He knew that if he got up to move around, he would somehow "break" whatever was happening to him. He lay quietly with his head in her lap, and a physical sensation of total ecstasy came over him.

"At the same time, I had a strange feeling of having come home," he said. "It was as if I were with someone that I had once known but hadn't seen for a long time—and never thought that I would see again."

The experience lasted for over an hour and a half. It was the most incredible experience that Bell and the woman (Semjase) had yet had in this lifetime.

"When I asked her who she was and where she was from, she told me that she would not yet tell me. She said not to worry about it, so I just continued to permit feelings to come to life within me. Old sensations were being rekindled. Emotions that had been suppressed through my entire life—feelings that I didn't think possible—were being reactivated.

"When I begged once more for her name and for more information about her, she only said that I would receive my answers in time from a distant land. I was left with that riddle until I read about the Billy Meier contact with Semjase in late 1979 or early 1980. From that time on, everything that Semjase promised has come to pass."

Being a contactee is not without its hazards. From time to time one might encounter some rather bizarre humanoid creatures and, according to Fred Bell, some entities that might be described as "energy scavengers."

"There are various disharmonic frequencies which are exchanged throughout the universe," he observed. "These 'energy scavengers' more or less clean things up. I once had an interaction with these entities, and they left me with a headache. It was not a comfortable exchange.

"On the other hand, I know a contactee who is much more in tune with these beings. I guess he must have a different kind of metabolic system than I do. He seems to be able to handle their energy field just fine."

"Fred," I wanted to know, "if a skeptic demanded of you your most conclusive proof that Semjase was a physical being and not a product of your imagination or the etheric world, what evidence would you provide?"

Bell's answer did not have to be contemplated. "I would provide absolutely nothing," he responded without hesitation. "To me, skeptics are the ones who created this negative world situation in which we presently exist. A skeptic is one who doesn't even believe in himself, let alone something else beyond himself. You can't convince a skeptic of life when he hasn't learned yet how to live."

Perhaps such an answer would not convince the Royal Academy of Science, but I could not help pondering my own question. *What would I accept as physical proof of Semjase's existence?* Unless she sat beside me on the sofa and I could see her spaceship hovering over Bell's home, what would convince me that Semjase had truly come from another planet?

How Do You Speak to a Spacewoman?

Fred Bell admitted that there were no witnesses who had seen him physically with Semjase. "Once there was an opportunity when friends had a chance to see her, and they all freaked out. This was back in 1972," he told me.

Semjase had admonished him that his friends' stress and excitement was a perfect example of why she must be cautious in her contacts with other people.

However, Fred said, he had had many witnesses observe the Pleiadean ships when he was communicating with them.

On one occasion in 1982, he was told by Semjase to bring a group of witnesses for a hillside encounter in

Laguna. He gathered up the people in his motor home and took them to the place that she had indicated.

Exactly at the time that Semjase had predicted, the ship came and did a series of maneuvers. Several witnesses saw this performance; and while the maneuvers were taking place, he told the people who were with him what would happen next. This was a very physical contact.

Once, when with Billy Meier, Semjase is said to have stumbled and severely injured her head, thus suggesting her physical vulnerability and her humanness.

Bell remembers when the accident happened, although he didn't know what happened until he read about it in a book, *UFO Contact from the Pleiades* by Lieutenant Colonel Wendelle C. Stevens (Ret.). "I think it was about 1978 or 1979, Billy and I were both having contacts with Semjase at that time. All of a sudden, for about the period of a year, I did not see her.

"I was certain I hadn't done anything to offend Semjase. Sometimes when I would make advances to her at different levels, she would be offended and move away for a period of time. My punishment for being too aggressive is usually a lack of contact, which leaves me in a lonely state. But during this time there was about a year's absence, and I wondered what happened to her. That accident was the reason for her absence.

"As far as Semjase's humanness, I am very convinced of it because of the feelings that we have had for each other and because of the powerful emotional exchanges that we have had."

In his contact experiences with Semjase, Fred has learned that her intellect is far greater than his. "She makes me look like a child, but I don't mind that. It's a great feeling to know that there are these powerful beings out there who, in turn, talk about beings over them who have the same relationship to them as the Pleiadeans do to us.

"We really can't look at power as a differentiating grid

between these different existences, but we have to look at the whole universal plan of evolution. A baby has the same amount of power as an adult—although to the ego, the adult would seem to be much more powerful than a child.''

Perceiving this from the spiritual level, there is an inner peace, an inner connection, that takes place in all of us and that is universal. Once we have learned to dissipate power throughout existence, it manifests itself as basically the same in everyone. However, the science of dissipating power and its energy takes some time to correlate, to apply in the proper manner, and to balance in our individual lifestyles.

We have the power to change our destiny every day. Each day the sun shines and a new day begins. Existence starts all over again. We have the complete ability to change our destiny, and we have the complete ability to break out of the patterns that others may impose upon us.

''Semjase has helped me with a lot of my systems, a lot of my scientific projects,'' Bell said. ''She has been very involved with them. When I make a mistake, it is very interesting because she really doesn't point it out, she lets me find it out for myself later.''

Semjase and Fred Bell had a deep physical and emotional experience in the very beginning of their relationship, and he is convinced that such interaction happened primarily to cement a bridge of contact between his previous lifetime and his prior existence in the physical with her. After that experience, Semjase told him that there would be no more of that kind of physical blending until he leaves the planet permanently.

It seems that Semjase is multidimensional in the same sense that we Earthlings are. All of us, when we reach a certain level of consciousness, become multidimensional—meaning that our consciousness can expand across many dimensions simultaneously, and can interact simultaneously.

The Tibetans teach us that in time we begin to walk and to balance ourselves between two worlds; the bridge across those two worlds is called the *antahkarana*. Semjase has the ability to serve as a bridge between two worlds.

"I can project into other people's imaginations. I have done it," Bell claimed. "People have seen me do it. Semjase does this as well, and that's something that we have in common.

"Semjase can do things that I can't do yet, because I have chosen to live this limited existence. She has come here to guide me and such has been our relationship for a long period of time, in this incarnation and in previous ones."

It is Fred's belief that Semjase began contacting him when he was just barely able to breathe on this planet, but that she remained always in the background. At the point where she felt he had become spiritually developed, she moved from the rear part of the picture to the front.

"We are very much in love in spirit," he professed. "Maybe someday Semjase will take an Earth-type incarnation, and I will remain space-born as she is now."

Could the alleged contact with Semjase be some kind of initiation process?

Though physical at first, Fred Bell stated, the contact with Semjase became much more mental. As it became increasingly mental, there were many misinterpretations of the Pleiadean messages. A lot of discipline was necessary to get the messages clear, to get the ego out of the way.

"Semjase isn't any sort of priestess," he said. "The Pleiadeans are just more educated than we are. They go to school for 120 years, so their educational level is higher.

"Humans have a way of looking at more evolved people as gods and goddesses and priests and priestesses, which really isn't the case. In her reality, Semjase is just an ordinary person.

"That's one thing the Pleiadeans stress in their messages: They're not to be considered as gods, and they would hope that we wouldn't even let that thought cross our minds.''

The Process of Selection

Fred Bell has said that he remembers being with the extraterrestrials before he was born. As he went through nursery school, he speculates that the frequency of contacts backed off because he had to start becoming more aware of the physical plane, but he had a lot of memories of his prior existences during nursery school times. The physical plane didn't feel comfortable to him at all, even then.

Later on when he was somewhere around eight or nine years old, he used to stand in fields in the countryside and look at the stars. He could hear conversations out there, and he could hear different civilizations.

Although he didn't have direct contact at that time, he was able to hear and to listen to extraterrestrial intelligences. Whenever he would get involved with the affairs of the Earth and the ways of humans, the higher presences would disappear or drift away.

In the late sixties and early seventies he went through a period of time studying with Tibetans, and he began to renew the awareness that he had more or less lost when he was in his early teens. Because he had renewed his energies in 1972, in 1973, when the physical contacts happened, he was prepared.

Is he concerned about his professional reputation when it becomes more widely known that he claims contact with an extraterrestrial?

"I've had to think long and hard about what I'm about to do, revealing this whole story of how I have had my own ten-year ongoing experience with UFOs. It's not that

I'm afraid to do it, it's just that I don't want to be thought of as trying to gain any kind of personal recognition by doing so. What I hope is that, by my opening up, a whole lot of people out there are going to have similar experiences. I'm going to disclose a knowledge that heretofore has not been opened up on this planet. I know that, and it's going to cause many positive changes."

Before Semjase makes contact with him, Fred feels a calm, then he feels like he is getting "high." It's an emotional, euphoric, upward feeling.

"This feeling of euphoria is very much more profound than the normal euphoric feelings that I would feel, say, from being down by the seashore or being in the mountains. This one supersedes any of that sort of thing.

"Then there is usually a kind of prickling on my neck. Sometimes the hairs on my arm will rise, even though I'm not cold. It's a sensation where the body hairs stand up because they are now transmitting electrical signals.

"I know why some of these things occur. For example, the euphoria is caused by a triggering of the neurohormone vasopressin, and this happens because the pituitary gland, which is the secretor of vasopressin, is hooked to the vagus nerve. The vagus nerve has a certain vibration, and because of the iron in the red blood cells, a coil network is formed as the blood flows through the particular pattern of the contactee's vagus nerve. Each vagus nerve in each individual has a separate or a distinct series of windings and turns on it."

The Pleiadeans are aware of the particular frequencies of his vagus nerve because they've been monitoring it since he was a child. Fred believes that they have influenced the shape of the nerve by the experiences that he has had, so that when they align their apparatus and their thought energies to that particular shape and that particular power, it resonates within him. The resonance, in turn, causes a harmonic response which then, of course, creates a physical sensation.

Fred is careful to emphasize that Semjase's transmissions to him are not his own thoughts being manipulated by his feelings. It's like somebody is inside of his head. There are words. There are voice qualities. There is a tone of voice, and then after that there are visual images—usually of Semjase, who is usually smiling.

Oftentimes there are other voices and other visual images, and his head becomes like a kind of television set. He can have his eyes open, looking straight ahead, yet still see a series of images apart from the outside world.

At the same time, he can communicate and look straight ahead and do whatever he is doing on a physical plane and still function coherently. He can be equally coherent in regard to his physical environment and to these visions and projections that are going on inside his head.

"I think that Semjase's most important message is that the people of Earth are not alone in the universe. We need to consider that there are, in fact, other intelligent civilizations," Fred stated. "In my mind, we are an unintelligent civilization in a galaxy of intelligent situations. That's the main message.

"Another message is that because, you know, we are the way we are—animalistic—that we are living on an isolated spaceship called Earth, and the environmental systems of this planet have only a limited life expectancy unless some preventative maintenance is performed. So I think their next message after the Number One message is that we are not taking care of ourselves spiritually or environmentally."

Semjase stresses environmental concerns. Horticulture is the main pastime of her home planet of Erra. There an entire civilization spends a great deal of time with nature, because it brings them to a higher awareness of the maintenance of the faculties of the environment in which they have been placed.

"The third message of the extraterrestrials is that they are willing to assist us," Fred added. "But until we digest the first two ideas, the third one isn't going to mean very much."

/emja/e Contact/ Another to Confirm Her Exi/tence

An interesting confirmation of Fred Bell's interaction with the entity Semjase comes from Sherry Hansen of Phoenix, who also claims a brief encounter with the Pleiadean.

It was about three years ago at a conference when an associate insisted that she meet Fred Bell. While attending his lecture, she was immediately struck by the amazing similarity in the content of his seminar to her own stress management workshops.

Their mutual thought patterns seemed to Sherry to be the obvious reason they were introduced. She was totally unsuspecting at the time that a life-altering experience would occur to her through Fred Bell . . . and someone very close to him.

Sherry comes from a very fundamental religious family. Her educational background is quite varied, with training in nursing and theology. She has had extensive and diverse experiences in counseling, community work, advertising, and the media, as well as in conducting stress management workshops. Her life has been embroidered with both silk and burlap, pleasure and pain, paradox upon paradox; yet with the hand of God guiding each stitch—no matter how separate the threads—a tapestry had been formed of the perfect lessons for a seeker of truth.

"I've walked a fairly straight and narrow road—but on that road have been many bumps and holes, tempered with several 'supernatural' experiences," she commented. "The one that I am about to describe would be one of the most meaningful."

About three or four months after meeting Fred Bell, the following occurred:

Upon coming out of a long meditation, Sherry heard a very melodic female voice speak to her, saying, "Sister, do not be frightened . . . I am Semjase."

There was a silent pause, and she felt a supreme peace. The voice continued: "In three days, Dr. Fred Bell will call you with a very important message."

"That was all," she recalled. "I can't say I saw anyone or anything. I still sat in the lotus position.

"I immediately shared the message with my daughter and a friend. I could see their reactions were similar to mine: This was something significant, albeit a bit mysterious . . . maybe even a little strange!

"I forgot about it. Then, three days later, Fred Bell called right on cue. I didn't know if I should tell him . . . or let him tell me. But being slightly overwhelmed, I told of the message."

Fred then said to her excitedly, "I don't know if you know that I am the 'unnamed contactee' in the UFO-Pleiadean books by Wendelle Stevens. I know *I* didn't tell you."

Sherry certainly did not know anything of this matter. Then Fred told her that for about two years he had had *no* contact with Semjase until three days earlier. At that time she had come to him with the message, "You must bring Sherry Hansen to the Firestar."

"Semjase actually *named* you," he said, his tone suggesting that he had had to recollect who this Sherry Hansen person was.

Fred went on to say that the whole thing was so profound that he and his wife would make arrangements to fly

Sherry in as soon as she could come—if she were willing. Well, indeed she was!

Fred underwent nearly a full day of preparations. He cleansed and purified the house, particularly the room where the experience would take place.

In the sixties and seventies, Sherry had produced a program called "Celebrate Life." A refined version of the presentation, tentatively named "Espiritus" (spirit of life), had been coming to her for many years. She had received much guidance and had done stacks of research and writing for the future show. In her projections for the program, she had incorporated the use of lasers and crystals and other new technologies to aid in the transmission of the message.

In Fred's living room was a huge crystal, together with lasers and pyramidal structures—all very close to what she had seen in visions ten to fifteen years earlier.

When all rituals, preparations, and cleansings had been performed, she was instructed to sit in a meditative pose and to go within herself.

"I remember looking into the crystal, as instructed, feeling at peace, but also having to deal with the thought that perhaps nothing would happen," Sherry said. "I prayed, and almost in a 'poof' I was gone. Somewhere.

"I have no Earthly memories for nearly five hours. As I left for 'somewhere,' I was met by a being of light and escorted through the most mystically beautiful experience of my life. No words can ever come close to describing what occurred.

"As audacious as this may sound to many, I truly felt as if in some way I saw or touched the Divine Force. The Light Being, a facet of the Divine Force, was so loving and caring and showed me so many things. The Being did not seem to have a gender, but I felt as though I knew him/her.

"It seemed as though we traveled through galaxies,

making stops along the way. There was one place—maybe it was a planet . . . maybe it was the New Jerusalem—where the beauty was far above anything I've ever dreamed possible. It was like a crystal/diamond planet, reflecting and refracting the purest, most brilliant colors. The light all around was effervescent. As a 'living crystal' I became fused with the light . . . I became the Light.

"Blissful elation permeated every cell of my beingness. I longed to have others experience this powerful love . . . this perfect love.

"I remembered Fred . . . and I tried to call out to him, to ask if he could see it also. But I knew that he could not hear me, because I couldn't use my 'body' mouth.

"Not long after that—or so it seemed—the Light Being told me that I had to go back. I was told that I would only remember a small part of what I had seen. More would be revealed to my conscious mind as I was able to share and to use the experience to help others."

With a jolt Sherry heard Fred firmly calling her name over and over. He had placed smelling salts under her nose.

Her body was numb. She felt disoriented, half in and half out of herself. Fred gave her some juice to ground her. She was not able to share much of the journey with him, but she remembers his sharing some of his observations.

"For three subsequent days I felt a little 'spacey' after the experience," Sherry stated. "Additional glimpses have gradually come back to me, and I *know* there is an absolute reality . . . a life beyond . . . a continuation of life . . . a perfect, all-encompassing power of love and peace, order and law. It is the love we are to be . . . it's the love we were . . . it's the love we are.

"More will be remembered by me when the time is right to share it. I bless and thank Semjase and Fred for a truly glorious gift."

Semjase as Archetype

Since this is a book of one startling theory and occurrence after another, it seems somehow appropriate to suggest a speculation that may appear very farfetched to some readers. Is it possible to see Semjase as a representation of the Great Mother archetype?

Let us begin with psychoanalyst Carl Jung's theory that within every man's unconscious there exists an anima. Often in dreams, or in a vision, the appearance to a man of a female "angel" may simply be his anima in disguise.

Within the past sixteen years, there has been an increasing number of reports concerning the appearance of a Great Mother image which, depending upon the witness, has been interpreted as the Virgin Mary, Pallas Athena, Isis, Diana, or simply the Blessed Mother. Are we witnessing the activation of a long-slumbering Goddess, the renewed manifestation of a universal archetype, or a kind of externalized anima of the collective unconscious? For as Jung would point out, when a female witness sees a female entity, she may be seeing simply an externalization of her "ideal self," as her own unconscious visualizes it.

There is no question about the power of the Great Mother archetype, and if such visions and apparitions and other feminine-intuitive, religiously oriented figures are increasing—and my correspondence and the research of my associates indicate that they are proliferating steadily on a global scale—we might then ask if certain parallels might be drawn between the contemporary interest in mysticism, the rise of the woman's liberation movement, and the appearance of such entities as Semjase.

I hardly think it coincidental that the Greek Muses, those entities who manifested themselves to inspire artists, poets, and thinkers, were always depicted as females. And isn't "necessity" the "mother" of invention?

Within our very souls it seems to be the feminine aspect that inspires, the masculine aspect that shapes and refines. And it seems likely that, from time to time, these facets of our souls may assume the archetypal images most suitable and most understandable to the individual who desires to manifest materially that which he or she creates mentally.

The balance of male and female is so essential to any meaningful creative expression that we would urge any business, any corporate structure, any committee of any kind to be certain to include a mix of men and women in any brainstorming session. In our present cultural expression it may still have to be the males who implement most plans, but they should never allow any residue of pride or any latent "macho" mentality to hinder them from accepting creative input from the females involved.

The Feminine-Creative Principle is deeply a part of each of us, and it must be given its proper due in our lives. The Holy Spirit is recognized as an expression of the feminine aspect of the Godhead. God the Father is the basic, the organizing and structuring principle in the Universe; but God the Mother is the creative energy that inspires all formulations required for the realization of thoughts, words, and deeds.

3

The UFO Prophets

On November 20, 1952, George Adamski walked into the night near Desert Center, California, and claimed to have communicated with a Venusian flying saucer pilot through telepathic transfer. The entity was benign and seemed concerned with the spiritual growth of humankind. He was what George Adamski called "a Space Brother."

Adamski was the first of our New Age UFO prophets; and interestingly, as the prophets of old had retreated into the desert wilderness to receive their inspiration, so had Adamski, by prearranged cosmic signal, gone to meet his Space Brother in the desert.

After 1952, there were several other men and women who declared contact with these concerned outer space beings. There was George Van Tassel, George Hunt Williamson, George King, Truman Bethurum, Daniel Fry, Cedric Allingham, Orfeo Angelucci, Franklin Thomas, Carl Anderson, Buck Nelson, John McCoy, Howard Menger, and Gloria Lee.

There are many individuals throughout the world who claim to have touched souls and, in some cases, bodies with Space Beings. Their accounts are circulated most often in privately printed books, which become scrolls of wisdom for thousands of questing seekers.

Flying-saucer literature ranges from accounts of fanciful adventures in other worlds, in which the contactee appears as some modern-day Gulliver being escorted through awesome alien cultures by an extraterrestrial guide, to works which concern themselves with more philosophical, religious, and moral information. The latter type reminds one of the prophetic imagery which was so often presented to the revelators in the Old Testament. It appears that there may be a basic transmission of spiritual knowledge that has bombarded this planet for centuries. In each new generation, the Big Broadcast seems to adapt itself to contemporary technology and the eccentricities of the current culture.

We must also note the difference between the contactee experience, such as that described by Fred Bell, and the more conventional UFO reports. The UFO literature contains accounts of men and women who became frightened or astonished when they had a sudden, unexpected encounter with an unknown aerial object or its occupants. These close encounters range from those in which the percipients sight "bug-eyed monster" types to those reported to involve "little green men."

The "bug-eyed monster" phenomenon may reveal something very atavistic in the psyche of humankind—the need always to be confronted by a fearful sentinel as one nears the brink in discovering an external goal or in the revelation of an aspect of the inner self. The "little green men" may represent the same kind of experience that people have had for centuries with what have been called "fairies" and "elves," for the miniature astronauts certainly conduct themselves in the traditional manner of the "wee people."

In the contactee literature, however, one reads the accounts of men and women who were not at all frightened by the attractive entities with whom they came into contact; men and women who, on the contrary, seem to have undergone a kind of cosmic consciousness experience.

UFOs in Laguna Canyon

A few years back, Fred Bell recounted, he was driving down Laguna Canyon at 2 A.M. There was a girl with him named Melanie who was half dozing off.

All of a sudden, it was as if a full moon had arisen. The whole canyon lighted up, and a huge disk came alongside of them on the left-hand side of the truck.

Melanie didn't see the disk directly, but she saw the flash. It was so bright that it woke her up from her sleep. The disk-shaped craft looked exactly like the moon with the exception that it followed them for about half a mile—then exploded and went straight up.

Fred remembered that the experience occurred about six months before the movie *Close Encounters of the Third Kind* came out.

"We came on home. I sat down at the keyboard and started playing music. It was 3 A.M., but I just felt a musical urge. I played this ascending thing, like the opposite of an arpeggio. An arpeggio is a descending keyboard maneuver that is very beautiful, very flowing. This was the opposite. It was stairsteps going up in sound.

"I recorded it. I have two witnesses. I have Melanie and Louise, the girl that I was living with at the time, who were both there while I played it.

"Six months later Spielberg came out with *Close Encounters of the Third Kind*. Remember when they're on top of Devils Tower, and they are playing music? Remember when the spaceship responds? I had recorded that soundtrack six months before the movie was released. I had no idea what I was doing. I just know this thing happened.

"I never did anything with the music, but the fact is, I performed it six months before the movie even came out."

Not too long ago, Fred continued, his wife Rowena was driving the car, and he was sitting on the passenger's side. He looked off to the right, and coming down Laguna Canyon was this big, bright flash.

The first thing he said to himself was that the way the canyon twists around, it could be either Jupiter or Venus. More likely Jupiter, because Jupiter was very predominant then, right below the moon at night.

But when he stared at it again, it had become a little more intense and had become brighter. Now he said, "Oh, I'm looking at the Orange County Airport."

Well, there happened to be an airliner coming in on what's called a "delayed flight path," meaning that the traffic pattern is busy and they have an outside pattern that just comes out to the edge of the canyon. So Fred decided that he was looking at the rotating beacon of probably a 734 AirCal jet. He was thinking as a scientist. Then the light got brighter and brighter, and he thought, "Well, this plane is really getting bright, and it's getting really close. It should be turning for its downwind leg, even on an extended path."

About that time the light started to accelerate toward the car, and Fred realized that for a minute and a half he had been watching the thing getting brighter and winding through the canyon.

Suddenly it was accelerating, and in ten seconds it was upon the car. It was brilliant. It flashed off, and he saw the outline of a Pleiadean beam ship.

It was Semjase, and Fred knew it only after a minute and a half!

"I got ten seconds of the total impact of what was happening—and then it was gone!

"Just as I realized what it was and I made a comment to Rowena, it was gone. It was history.

"That's what I call teasing, you know what I mean? But at the same time, the message was 'Always be on guard. Always keep yourself in a state to be receptive to that energy.'"

A UFO Appearance on Schedule

At Christmas in 1980, Semjase said that she would give Fred a special present. She told him on Christmas Day what the present would be: a close encounter that could be witnessed by friends.

Semjase said that he should tell his best friends, those whom he considered to be worthy, that they would have the experience at a certain point in Laguna.

"We were having a Christmas party up in Los Angeles in Bel Air, so I grabbed some of my friends and we got in my motor home," Fred explains.

"We went down to this mountain that's on the backside of where I live now. We were at about 2200 feet. There were no residences nearby. The view was toward San Diego across millions of acres of vacant land that constitute the Marine Base down in San Diego, starting with the outside of the El Toro Base up here."

Semjase came in with what is called a *Variation 4 Beam Ship* and stopped at two thousand, maybe three thousand feet over the ground and approximately two miles away.

Fred asked her telepathically why she was so far away, and she replied that the crew was going to demonstrate the propulsion system of the craft. It would be hazardous to be too close because of the electrostatic charges.

He asked her, "What about radar? Aren't you going to be seen on radar?"

She answered, "No, because it's 1 A.M. Christmas night. Every single person on the radar sets is not watching the radar scopes at this time, because this is an evening when military forces just aren't paying attention to details. It's a holiday, and it's a sacred holiday."

The spacecraft then executed what is called a "punch-out," where the ship accelerates at a vertical speed of about 18,000-some-odd mph. This speed is just around the escape velocity from a point about a mile high straight out into space. The craft performed this three times.

Each time, at approximately minute-and-a-half intervals, the ship would go straight up.

"I would say that in about four seconds the craft was one hundred miles out there. Then it would accelerate back down, and as it came down, it would take about a minute and a half.

"The downward motion of the spaceship is a falling leaf kind of movement. You know, the way an oak leaf will kind of float back and forth as it drops from the branch.

"When the ship went up it produced a curtain of light, like the aurora borealis, so we could see this series of mushrooming lights. The whole quadrant, like one eighth of the sky, was lit up."

Semjase explained that this was the negative ionization effect created by the propulsion system of the ship. The negative ions were actually healing the atmosphere of the pollutants in a large sector.

Fred asked her, "Why don't you bring more ships in here and clean up the atmosphere for all of us?"

She responded, "We can't, because of the way Earth humans respond. If we *were* to do such a cleansing, they would have a tendency to make the atmosphere even dirtier, not respecting what was going on."

Fred totally agreed.

After Semjase's ship had repeated its maneuvers three times and left, Fred's friends were flabbergasted. He had told them during the day what time and where and what the effect was going to be, and it had actually happened. The experience was so good that people talked about it for weeks and weeks.

From what Fred understands, there have been only two such demonstrations in all of the series of contacts that anybody knows have happened. One here in the United States for him, and the other in Switzerland for Billy Meier.

Semjase once said, and this is a quotation to Meier, "In the course of our duties, we do here and there approach denizens of various worlds, select some individuals and communicate with them. This we do only when it raises the higher state of evolution. Then we explain to them that they are not the only thinking beings in the universe."

Fred is fond of saying that Semjase, even though she is a gentle-looking female, intellectually blows him away in about two microseconds. "Her level of intellect is so far beyond mine, I feel like a blithering idiot sometimes."

Once in a while Semjase gets quite stern and quite harsh. She feels that most Earthlings prefer to turn their brains off, rather than to give them the minimal exercise of thought. Those inclined to be skeptical would not believe in the reality of extraterrestrial life if a ship landed on their porch.

Semjase has told Fred that Earth people who are negative are labelled as having an "auric stench." An auric stench is a distasteful phrase which describes the negative energies that emanate from Earth humans, often without their knowledge or conscious thought. These frequencies create a state of altered equilibrium in a Pleiadean being, and for this reason are monitored carefully.

How Do They Fly?

Semjase has told Fred much about the Pleiadeans' technology, and he has even operated one of the craft by remote control from the ground level. He has his notes from a conversation on Mother's Day, 1980, that explain some interesting aspects of their space vehicles.

Semjase and he were talking about their propulsion systems and fire, because he had noticed the particular glow that they have.

She said, "Our spaceships, though physical, become living flames in flight. When you fly the astral plane, both sides are pure."

"What that means," Fred clarified, "is that when you accelerate consciousness or when you accelerate anything up beyond the speed of light, you immediately transmute over to the astral plane."

When Semjase said "both sides are pure," she meant that there is a purification process on the astral plane. The entities there are not as gross as they are here on this plane.

According to Semjase, "Both good and evil dwell in deep space denizens. Only purpose is a sign of progress. We fly with purpose, and when we lose it, as in old age, it is immediately regained by the Super Soul of the Universe. Our individuality is never lost. Whether we work for God or against God, it matters not, for we are all of God—and our forms preserve our Karmic quest in search of the unmanifest."

At this point Fred asked Semjase what happens when the Pleiadeans die.

As Semjase explained it, each one of her people has a mission in life. The ones who fly in ships around the universe are regarded as pioneers. When the pilots attain a certain age, such as eight hundred or nine hundred years old, the ship may be destroyed because of miscalculations. At that time, the entities go into the Super Soul. They become part of everything.

The UFO as Deliverer

Very often UFO contactees are, by their own admission, individuals who have become disillusioned with the existing religious institutions and dissatisfied with contemporary social and economic injustices. As in the accounts of the prophets of old, the contemporary contactees are seeking a more intimate relationship with a source of strength and inspiration outside of themselves.

After the contact experience, these world-weary pilgrims claim to have received this spiritual succor from Space Beings. The contactees feel that their questions have been answered and that their quest has come to an end. They have become messengers for a new gospel.

However one deals with the Flying Saucer Movement in one's own reality, the undeniable fact remains that thousands of men and women throughout the world have made the UFO a symbol of religious awakening and spiritual transformation. Some envision the UFO as their deliverer from a world fouled by its own inhabitants.

Who is attracted to the message of the UFO contactee? And do such seekers stabilize their lives and attain redemption and/or spiritual elevation? Or do they find only a transient sense of community before sliding back into mental confusion in a dark chaos of the soul?

Of keen interest to religionists, social scientists, and psychologists, as well as to the average person, is how numerous men and women are able to utilize their UFO ecclesiasticism in a positive way and to function as totally integrated individuals in today's complex modern society.

There is an enormous amount of New Age revelatory material which has been given to the UFO contactees by the alleged occupants of interstellar, multidimensional space-craft. Many of these revelations warn of impending Earth changes and indicate a frightful Armageddon. Hope is offered if certain stipulations are fulfilled by errant Earth-lings. The Space Age Apocrypha is proliferating in the 1980s.

Are the UFO contactees disciples of a New Age religion which will offer a blending of technology and traditional spiritual concepts? Or have they assumed their shepherds' staffs and acquired an anxious flock before they "got themselves together" on their own vision quest?

Our Friends from the Pleiades

The Pleiades were so important to the ancient Greek civilization, Fred Bell stated, that at least six temples were built wholly oriented toward these stars. From these temples, the stars of the gods were watched.

At some unknown date, perhaps contemporaneous with those Grecian structures, the Pleiades were pictured in the New World upon a blue background on the walls of the Palenque temple. Certainly the Pleiades were well known in parts of Mexico. In 1519, Cortez found that there was a very ancient tradition of the destruction of the world in some past age that was associated with the Pleiades.

Here in North America, we can point out Steven Spielberg's use of the Devils Tower in connection with UFOs in *Close Encounters of the Third Kind*. The Devils Tower is an American legend, and we find that the Pleiades were connected with it.

The Kiowa Indians call it *Mateo Tepe*; and according to their tradition, the tower was raised by the Great Spirit to protect seven Indian maidens who were pursued by giant bears. The maidens were afterward placed in the sky as the Pleiades cluster, and to this day the marks of the bears' claws may be seen as the vertical striations on the side of the tower. The Cheyenne Indians had a similar legend.

Every civilization on the face of the Earth has had some kind of an experience with the Pleiades, the "seven sisters."

In Mexico at the sacred site of Ticohuoten some twenty-eight miles north of Mexico City, the west face of the Great Pyramid of the Sun is oriented to the setting of the Pleiades, and eleven of the west-running streets of the city point to the same spot on the horizon. These structures are even more ancient than the Aztec or Toltec cultures, by the way.

In the Caribbean Islands the Pleiades are considered by the Cunas to be the location of the exact center of heaven, the house where the Creator of the Universe lives. The Cunas also say that the Pleiades constitute the soul of God.

In *Secrets of the Cuna's Earth Mother* by Clyde Keeler, there was a quotation that states, "It seems as though there is a constant struggle going on in the sky between the people of light and goodness and the people of darkness and evil. Ikwaniktipippi, in describing certain celestial bodies, referred to this battle. He spoke of the Pleiades as seven heroes who are arrow makers who prepare fiery shafts for the battle. At other times, the Pleiades constitute the soul of God where God lives."

The Yellow Emperor of China, Huang-ti, who is said to have lived between approximately 2997 and 2587 B.C., is considered by many of the Taoists to be a miraculous being who succeeded in attaining immortality. During his reign, utensils of wood, clay, and metal were manufactured; boats and carts were constructed and utilized; and the medium of currency was originated. Provinces of the vast country were mapped. Acupressure and acupuncture became sciences. The Emperor is generally acknowledged as the father of holistic medicine, and Huang-ti himself claimed that much of his rapid development began because of conversations held in court with his consultants, who were supposedly beings from the Pleiades.

The Hopi Indians named the Pleiades *Huhokan*, meaning "Those who cling together." They, too, consider themselves to be direct descendents of the inhabitants of the Pleiades.

The Hopi, as well as the Navajo and several other cultures throughout the world, use star calendars to allow them to chart the seasons and special events. The system they used was based on a 260-day, sacred round, or minor, cycle; and a 365-day major cycle, which equalled a period between midnight culminations of the Pleiades. Any day calculated on these cycles could not repeat itself for 18,980 days or 52 years.

In the sacred Kiva of Mesas, the Hopi ceremoniously light the new fire. This appears every fifty-two years when the temple's sacred points align with the stars. All fires are extinguished throughout the nation and rekindled from a sacred fire produced by the holy men.

The young men of the tribe learn the importance of the Pleiades early in life. Initiation into the spiritual ways takes place only when the cherished cluster is directly overhead at night.

Fred Bell has a certain area in his home where he burns candles tied into the Hopi system. "They have a tremendous amount of power. They burn twenty-four hours a day, seven days a week. I've done this for over ten years in the same position, and I've never let them go out. It's a discipline, but at the same time the act enforces my consciousness constantly to elevate and to proceed forward. You don't really go backward with this kind of discipline.

"The Indians were totally into this sort of thing. The Iroquois believed the twinkling orbs represent seven young people who guard the holy sky throughout the night, and they have prayers for happiness addressing them."

Earth needs to realize that it's in trouble, Fred commented. If help is given to this planet at this stage, it will absolutely be a worthless gesture. Help from the Pleiadeans might temporarily alleviate certain problems as they are now, but it would not alleviate the conditions that led the problems into existence.

What has to happen is that Earth people have to get sicker. The planet has to get worse and worse until a lot of the people who helped create this mess are discarded out of their physical bodies. Earth people must finally wake up and realize what's going on and make some effort to correct things. At such a time, the Pleiadeans can help.

Assistance on a planetary level will not occur until all nations put a stop to war. These foolish squabbles that are going on in the Middle East will have to cease. All territorial and boundarial disputes will have to end. Earth will have to unite and to recognize that its problem is not the state of its internal boundaries, but the reality of its boundaries with the edge of space. Then the Pleiadeans can help, but not until that time.

Through Semjase, Fred has learned of the Andromeda Council that works with the Council of the Elders.

"There are confederations, not necessarily of planets, but of groups that travel like the Pleiadeans, such as the people that live on Lyra. There is a common brotherhood throughout the cosmos, and that's the way the whole universe is structured."

The human race has total freedom to build itself into any level it wants—or to destroy itself.

The Pleiadeans are not manipulating us at all, Fred insisted. As a matter of fact, when they come into our world, they usually don't stay more than two or three hours in this dimension because the atmosphere is so bad, the pollution is so bad, that it affects them.

The human race has its free hand over itself. God, of course, will intervene if certain matters arise.

Our spiritual bodies preside over us as protectors. Depending on how enlightened we are, we can have a tremendous determination on how much of an effect we have—through our higher nature—over our own destinies.

4

The Contactee Experience

Ever since 1967 I have been conducting a serious study of certain contactees, whom I call "flying-saucer missionaries," and I have noted that a considerable percentage of the information dispensed in their cosmic sermonettes has contained a good deal of accurate information and that several of their predictions have been realized.

In my opinion, many UFO researchers—and nearly all the news media and the orthodox scientists—have been too hasty in their assessments that the contactees' messages are just so much nonsense and science-fiction-inspired, pseudo-religious prattle. Although several of the contactees seem to parrot in a tedious manner a great amount of the same basic "message," we might discover important clues hidden for us in their fanciful distortions if only we were to work a bit harder to separate the cosmic wheat from the celestial chaff.

The flying-saucer contactees are convinced that they are in direct communication with "space intelligences" through telepathic thought transference. In cases such as Fred Bell's, the contactee also claims a personal and physical confrontation with a beneficent "Space Being," who originated the contact; but by the time I, or any other researchers I know, have arrived on the scene, the contactee is receiving his messages solely via "mental telepathy."

There does seem to be a heightening, after the contact experience, of what one would normally consider manifestations of extrasensory perception. In one instance, for example, I had a contactee describe my home in exceptionally minute detail while we sat in a room several hundred miles away. Along with such demonstrable clairvoyant abilities, the contactee is often left with a timetable of certain predictions of future events.

In spite of such setbacks as unfulfilled prophecies, a good many of the contactees continue to be imbued with an almost religious fervor to spread the message that has been given to them by the Space Beings. The zeal with which these flying-saucer missionaries desire to preach the cosmic gospel must surely remind one of the early Apostles, who were given the divine mission to "go quickly and tell."

A distillation of the Outer Space Apocrypha would reveal such concepts as the following:

- *Humankind is not alone in the solar system. "Space brothers and sisters" have come to Earth to reach and to teach those humans who will respond to the promise of a larger universe.*

- *The Space Beings have advanced information which they wish to impart to their weaker brethren. They want humankind to join an intergalactic spiritual federation.*

- *The Space Beings are here to teach, to help awaken the human spirit, to help humankind rise to higher levels of vibration so that the people of Earth may be ready to enter new dimensions.* (According to the Outer Space Apocrypha, such a goal was precisely what Jesus, the prophets, Confucius, and the other leaders of the great religions have tried to teach humanity.)

• *Humankind stands now in the transitional period before the dawn of a New Age.* (With peace, love, and understanding, the people of Earth will see a great new era begin to dawn.)

• *If the Earthlings should not raise their vibratory rate within a set period of time, severe earth changes and major cataclysms will take place.* (Such disasters will not end the world, but shall serve as cataclysmic crucibles to burn off the dross of unreceptive humanity. Those who die in such dreadful purgings will be allowed to reincarnate on higher levels of development so that their salvation will be more readily accomplished through higher teachings on a higher vibratory level.)

How do our flying-saucer contactees, our apostles of intergalactic peace and harmony, receive their "tongues of flame"? Here again a definite pattern has emerged in both my own research and in the investigations of others:

• *The contactees saw the UFO on the ground, hovering low overhead, or heard a slight humming sound above them which drew their attention to a mysterious craft.*

• *A warm ray of "light" emanated from the craft and touched the contactees on the neck, the crown of the head, or the middle of the forehead. In certain instances, the contactees may have lost consciousness at this point and, upon awakening, may have discovered that they could not account for anywhere from a minute or two to an hour or two of their time.* (Those contactees who claim communication with Space Beings generally have no recollection of any period of unconsciousness, but they maintain that they "heard" a voice speaking to them from inside their own heads. In either case, whether consciousness is retained or lost, the contactee usually experiences a slight "tingling" sensation before the contact proper.)

• *The contactees who retained consciousness and communicated with either an attractive Space Being or a "voice" inside their head have very often been told that they were selected because they were, in reality, someone very special.* (Many contactees are told that they are reincarnations of notable world figures of the past. A good number are informed that they really are aliens, who were planted on Earth as very small children.)

• *All types of contactees seem to have suffered through several days of restlessness, irritability, sleeplessness, and unusual dreams or nightmares immediately after the initial contact experience. Many have reported noticing a terrible thirst after the departure of the entity.*

• *After a period of a week to several months, the contactee who has received a cosmic charge to spread the Space Beings' message feels prepared to go forth and preach the word.* (I have had previously tongue-tied and painfully shy people beg me to use whatever influence I might possess so that they could lecture before auditoriums filled with people. The contactees, in many instances, seem especially driven to seek lecture tours on college campuses.)

• *None of the flying-saucer missionaries seem to feel any fear of their solar brothers and sisters.* (Most of them look forward to a return visit from the Space Beings, and the majority of them have been promised repeated contacts.)

• *Family and friends of the contactee report that he is literally a different and changed person after his alleged experience.* (Higher intelligence and perception are often mentioned, as well as a seeming increase in ESP or psychic abilities.)

Why are so many men and women forsaking jobs, families, and respectability in order to preach the cosmic New Testament of the Space Beings?

Is an as-yet-undetermined *someone* systematically selecting certain individuals for some worldwide program of psychological conditioning?

Can it really be true that aliens from other worlds seek to program these flying-saucer missionaries in an effort to raise humankind's propensity to believe, and its capacity to love and understand?

Has some as-yet-unidentified agency set in motion an extensive propaganda campaign which has been designed to prepare the whole of humankind for a dramatic confrontation with an alien race or culture?

As a result of my own investigations and the research of others, I can no longer doubt that such "contacts" are taking place on a global scale; but I must challenge certain of the UFO occupants, especially in regard to their place of origin—that is, outer space.

I do not dogmatically rule out the extraterrestrial hypothesis, but I do lean toward the theory that UFOs may be our neighbors right around the corner in another space–time continuum. What we have thus far been labeling "spaceships" may be, in reality, multidimensional mechanisms or psychic constructs of our paraphysical companions.

I have even come to suspect that, in some instances, what we have been terming "spaceships" may actually be a form of higher intelligence, rather than vehicles transporting occupants.

I feel, too, that these intelligences have the ability to influence the human mind telepathically in order to project what may appear to be three-dimensional images to the witnesses of UFO activity. The image seen may depend in large part upon the preconceptions which the witness has about alien life forms; and thus our reported accounts of occupants run the gamut from Bug-eyed Monster types to Little Green Men to Metaphysical Space Brothers.

The mechanism employed by the UFO entities is always relevant to the witness's time context. At the same time, the form in which the UFO construct appears—and the symbology it employs—are always timeless, archetypal, and instantly recognizable at one level of the beholder's consciousness. Elves, fairies, and angelic beings, it would seem, have been popular in all cultures and in all recorded time. The complete experience of any witness to UFO activity is quite probably part of a natural process whose actual purpose is simply too staggeringly complex for our desperately throbbing brains to deal with at this moment in time and space.

It seems to me that the UFO entities may have been fibbing to us about their true identity and their true place of origin since our earliest antiquity. On the other hand, I must concede that it may well be that we are being slowly provided with the bits and pieces of some supercosmic jigsaw puzzle, which one day, when properly assembled, will give us the complete picture of the entire UFO enigma.

Becoming a Candidate for Contact

Aleuti Francesca, "Telethought Channeler" for the Solar Light Center in Central Point, Oregon, has communicated with Space Beings since 1954.

In Aleuti's opinion, one must use the utmost caution in dealing with the mystery of contact.

"One should never inform the press, radio or TV people of his contact and nothing at all should be publicized until, or unless, at least one major prophecy has come true for a specific date and has thus established the accuracy of the source. A great deal of harm can come of several neophyte channelers running about the country crying 'wolf' in regard to the sinking of lands, and so forth. So many of these prophecies with nonfulfilled dates have plagued the Space and psychic field of late, and they cause intelligent people to turn away in disgust."

Aleuti also warns of the danger of "astral entities" masquerading as Space Beings.

"This is not uncommon lately in the psychic field," she said, "but it is rarely that I have known Space people to make contacts through Ouija boards or some other such device. So many young people know nothing of astral impersonators or unconscious fraud and they cannot see that what they are doing is not what it seems."

The following is Aleuti's advice to those who wish to attempt telepathic or physical contact with the Space Brothers:

"I will no longer suggest or recommend interested people attempting such contacts unless they are willing to put themselves through a specific kind of program of *self-discipline* and *self-knowledge*. Over the last few years I have observed such juvenile antics and ego-inflation taking place in untrained and unprepared mentalities as to be downright dangerous, both to the cause and to the individuals themselves.

"If the Space intelligences want to contact you, they will do so; *they* do the choosing."

Then for those who might desire to make themselves fit candidates for contact, she presented the following questions and comments:

1. Have you dedication of a spiritual nature?
2. Have you courage to stay with your convictions without bravado, quietly, reasonably, *peacefully*?
3. Do you really know yourself inside and out, through hell and high water? If not, start a self-knowledge program.
4. Have you an inferiority complex or a secret desire for power? If so, forget about Space people and go to work to balance your ego and attain inner poise. When you truly know self, you will find knowledge of others follows.

   The Space Brothers need highly *stable* individuals. Are you one?

   Astral interlopers, masquerading as Space intelligences, clutter up the Space field. They flourish in the purely psychic realm. They feed on vanity and ego. Organizations have even been formed around power-mad individuals claiming Space contacts from such sources. BE ALERT! BE AWARE!

   Space men and women from the Solar and Galactic

Confederations are concerned with the *good of all peoples*, of any nationality on Earth, whom they can reach. They preach no dogmas nor creeds, nor do they feed "ego food" to their channels. All *true* channels are part of a *plan to assist the Earth* and its peoples through the *great change* or initiation. Some play a greater part, some a lesser, but all are part of the Plan, Cosmic and spiritual in nature. The desire to serve, to love, and to understand is the real mark of a *true* Light server. "By their deeds shall ye know them."

Principles of the Solar Light Center

1. *Belief in an Infinite Creator (the All-Knowing-One, of the Space Beings) and in the Cosmic Christ, the Spiritual Hierarchy, and the Great White Brotherhood.*

2. *Belief in the expression of universal love, compassion, and understanding as the true basis for world peace and the healing of all humankind's ills.*

3. *Acceptance of the eternal truths given by World Atavars (Jesus, Buddha, Krishna) and spiritual Masters as taught in most esoteric schools of thought.*

4. *Belief that other planets are inhabited by advanced beings who have attained mastery over space travel, hence they are called Space Beings.*

5. *Belief in communication with advanced Space Beings by such means as direct physical contact, telethought, telepathy, tensor beam, light beam, and other means.*

6. *Belief that a spiritual Light is being sent to uplift the Earth and raise the frequency level of all cells, all atoms, in preparation for the coming change, and this Light can be focused through certain Light Centers in Vortex areas.*

7. *Belief that our Freedom of Attitude toward: (1) the Infinite Creator, (2) Self (ego), (3) other beings, is the deciding factor on the path to the All-Highest,*

and service in the Universal Program is the key to this.

8. *Belief that as the end of a Great Cycle of approximately 26,000 years approaches, a ''cleansing'' is taking place due to Light energies received, and the planet is being prepared for a density level transition into a higher frequency.*

5

The Flying /aucer Movement

Most contactees would agree that although the Space Beings' technology is dazzling, their prominent characteristic is wisdom.

The contactees seem to take the Space Beings' scientific knowledge for granted. After all, if they have traveled through space from other worlds to Earth, then they must quite obviously be extremely and sublimely intelligent.

Hard-nosed Earth scientists, however, remain singularly unimpressed with the specific technical information that has been relayed by the contactees.

One might argue that either the UFOnauts deem their science to be incomprehensible to humankind at this point, or that they are not at all concerned with relaying technical data which might make humankind even more baffled and beset by machines and technology than it already seems to be.

Other theorists might state that the contactees are not contacting alien entities at all, but, rather, a higher aspect of their own psyches, perhaps the pure essence that is free of the mundane limitations of time and space and is able to tap a kind of universal, cosmic reservoir of wisdom.

George Van Tassel was told by his contact, Ashtar, that the Space Beings' purpose was to save humankind from itself. Once that great obstacle has been met, then the minor problem of how to deal with nuclear fission will right itself through the harmony that will then be extant on the planet Earth.

The Space Beings seem very concerned with the spreading of what has come to be known as New Age concepts— fresh methods of looking at metaphysics, universal laws, brotherhood, and even health and hygiene. The Space Beings appear definitely concerned with seeing that all humankind is united as ''one'' on this planet.

Angels from Outer Space

There seems little question that the Space Beings function as the angels once did. They are concerned about Earth. They seem to be actively trying to protect it and the people in it. They are powerful. They avoid, or have control over the physical limitations of time and space, yet they are benevolent and kindly disposed toward fumbling, bumbling, ineffectual humankind.

It seems either that Space Beings have placed themselves in the role of messengers of God, or that we, in our desperation for cosmic messiahs who can remove us from the foul situation we have made on this planet, hope that there *are* such messengers who can extricate us from the plight we have brought upon ourselves.

Space Beings as Spirit Guides

Although most of the contactees claim an initial physical contact with a Space Being, the operable mechanics of the experience seem very reminiscent of what we have come to see in Spiritualism as the medium working with a Spirit guide or a control from the "other side." In Spiritualistic or mediumistic channeling, we are familiar with the psychic sensitive who goes into various depths of the trance state and who relays information through the guide, who contacts various spirits of deceased human personalities. The mechanism in the Flying Saucer Movement is very often that of the contactee going into some state of trance and channeling information from Space Beings.

George King, George Van Tassel, Gloria Lee, George Hunt Williamson, and several other contactees have been members of psychic development groups, a fact which many skeptics have attempted to use to discredit their subsequent contacts with alleged beings from other worlds.

At the same time, though, it should not really be so surprising to consider that men and women who have lived their lives devoted to a mystical quest might one day be presented with a demonstrable realization of their search. We do not find it suspect, for example, when devout young people, who were reared in deeply religious families and attended parochial schools, very often become priests, rabbis, nuns, or missionaries. Therefore it would seem that men and women who all of their lives have been predisposed toward psychic development should not necessarily be criticized for later having undergone meaningful visionary experiences.

By the 1960s, few people were claiming the kind of direct physical contact that George Adamski had alleged had been his on the desert, and the "psychic-channeling saucer groups" were becoming increasingly approved by the faithful. The career of Gloria Lee, a former airline stewardess and wife of aircraft designer William H. Byrd, is somewhat typical of the type of channeling popular in the 1960s.

Ms. Lee had seen a UFO in the early 1950s. In 1953, she began to receive telepathic communications from a man of Jupiter who revealed himself as "J.W."

As Gloria Lee came to place more confidence in her Space Being, she became a well-known figure among UFO cultist groups as a lecturer and a channel. J.W. revealed that on Jupiter vocal cords had gone out of use, so he began to write a book through Gloria Lee. He also led her to found The Cosmon Research Foundation, dedicated to the spreading of his teachings and the bringing about of man's spiritual development in preparation for the New Age. Through his direction and the persistence of Gloria Lee on the lecture circuit, the Foundation became a thriving organization and a second book appeared.

Then, tragically, Gloria Lee starved herself to death after a sixty-six-day fast instituted upon the instructions of her mentor from Jupiter. The fast was carried out in the name of peace, in a Gandhi-like effort to make the United States government officially investigate and study plans for a spacecraft that Ms. Lee had brought with her to Washington.

Gloria Lee secured herself in a hotel room on September 23, 1962. On December 2, with still no word from the government officials—or from her Space Being—the thirty-seven-year-old contactee died.

Shortly after her passing, the Mark-Age Metacenter in Miami, Florida, announced that they were receiving communications from Gloria Lee in the spirit world. The etheric form of Miss Lee told the group that she was now able to find out how the method of interdimensional communication, by which she said her two books had been written, actually worked.

As the Metacenter took notes for a booklet Gloria Lee's publisher would later issue to the faithful and the curious, Gloria's spirit spoke through the channel, Yolanda; it explained how her conscious intelligence had been transferred to another frequency, another body, of higher vibrational rate.

In the twenty-four years since Gloria Lee made her transition to another vibration, the Flying Saucer Movement has seen the formation and continuation of dozens of groups, which present their followers with regular messages from the Space Beings. Many of them have, like Mark-Age, grown directly out of the old theosophical I AM frame of reference. Others have grown up around individual contactees who channel their own teachings.

Mark-Age Metacenter of Miami was chartered by the state of Florida on March 27, 1967. Founders of the Center were Mark, Astrid, Wains, Zan-thu, and the major channel, Yolanda.

Sananda has become a popular name for Jesus in the Flying Saucer Movement, and, according to Mark-Age, Jesus has been in orbit around the planet since 1885 and will take on material form as Earth's transition to a higher consciousness is made. Mark-Age has recently acquired several acres of land in California, and is expanding its publishing program, which has already turned out a number of books in the Flying Saucer Movement.

The Enigma of Adam/ki

The death of George Adamski on April 12, 1965, by no means terminated the heated controversy which had never stopped swirling around the prolific and articulate contactee. Adamski, too, was quickly resurrected by his followers. In the book *Scoriton Mystery* by Eileen Buckle, a contactee named Ernest Bryant claims to have met three spacemen on April 24, 1965, one of whom was a youth named Yamski, whose body already housed the reincarnated spirit of George Adamski.

Throughout his career as a contactee, Adamski's believers steadfastly declared him to be one of the most saintly of men, completely devoted to the teachings of universal laws. It appears that after his death, certain of his followers found it necessary to provide their discipline of intergalactic peace with a kind of instant resurrection.

According to Desmond Leslie, George Adamski had an audience with Pope John just a few days before the Pope passed away. Leslie says that he met Adamski at the airport in London just after the controversial contactee had flown in from Rome. He drove Adamski straight to his little river cruiser at Staines where several people interested in UFOlogy had been spending the weekend.

Sometime during the next few days, Adamski showed Leslie a memento that he said no one would ever take from him, and he produced an exquisite gold medal with Pope John's effigy on it. Later Leslie checked and found it was a medal which had not yet been released to anyone.

When Adamski was asked how he had received it, he answered that Pope John had given it to him the day before. Adamski went on to say how he had arrived at the Vatican according to the space people's instructions and had been taken straight in, given a cassock, and led to the Pope's bedside.

It was here that Adamski had handed Pope John a sealed package from the Space Brothers. It was said that Pope John's face had beamed when he received the package, and he said, "This is what I have been waiting for!" The Pope then presented Adamski with a very special medal, and the papal audience ended.

Leslie said that he later checked with Lou Zinstag, who it was said had taken Adamski to the Vatican. Ms. Zinstag reported that when they had approached the Vatican and neared the private entrance, a man with "purple at his throat" (apparently a monsignor or a bishop) appeared.

Adamski had cried out, "That's my man!", greeted the papal official, and was led in for an audience with the Pope. Ms. Zinstag said that when he reappeared about twenty minutes later, Adamski appeared to be in the same state of excitement and rapture as witnesses had described him being in after his desert contact with the Space Brothers in 1952.

When Leslie later asked an abbot he knew about the medal, the clergyman was amazed and said that such a medal would only have been given to someone in the most exceptional circumstances, and that no one, so far as he knew, had yet received this particular medal.

Leslie conceded that he had initially disbelieved that Adamski had received such an audience with the Pope, but this confirmation from the abbot with regard to the medal had overcome his former disbelief.

When Leslie asked Adamski what the Space Brothers' package had contained, the contactee said that he did not know. He said that it had been given to him by the Space Brothers before he had left for Europe and that he had been given instructions to give it to the Pope. He was also told that all arrangements had been made inside the Vatican for such an audience to take place. This suggested to Leslie that the Space Brothers have a "fifth column" in St. Peter's seat as well as everywhere else.

Adamski told Leslie that he thought the package had contained instructions and advice for the second ecumenical council. It is possible that the package also contained a message to the Big Fisherman's successors which chided them about certain lax measures and encouraged them to get on with the serious work required on the Earth plane.

George Hunt Williamson was the author of a number of books concerning archaeological evidence for early extraterrestrial visitation. Williamson (who died in January 1986) formed the Brotherhood of the Seven Rays under the tutelage of an entity who revealed himself as Ascended Master Araru-Muru. The Outer Retreat was established by Williamson, who then called himself Brother Philip, at an abbey near Lake Titicaca.

As the name Brotherhood of the Seven Rays implies, it hoped to encompass all the Theosophical virtues symbolized as rays of light. Through its Ancient Amethystine Order, it focused on the violet rays, symbol of the present movement of the Earth.

Commandant Ashtar

George Van Tassel published his first booklet in 1952 and introduced the world to "Ashtar, commandant of station Schare." *Schare* is said to be one of several saucer stations in Blaau, the fourth sector of Bela, into which our solar system is moving. "Shan" was the name that Van Tassel's contact gave for planet Earth. Van Tassel's Ashtar also decreed the universe to be ruled by the Council of Seven Lights, which had divided the Cosmos into sector systems and sectors.

Van Tassel founded the Ministry of Universal Wisdom based on his revelations of the Space Brothers. This ministry teaches the universal law which operates on humankind in seven states: *gender* (male and female); the creator as *cause*; *polarity* of negative and positive; *vibration*; *rhythm*; *relativity*; and *mentality*.

Van Tassel maintained his headquarters at Giant Rock, California, for many years. He made it a gathering place for both the curious and the true believers.

Contacts Continue

It is impossible to estimate how many men and women are receiving messages from Space Beings. Groups continue to rise from dynamic contactees, each with their variations of previous revelations and their own occasional individual input.

There is also the category of revelators which UFOlogists term the "silent contactees"—men and women who have not gathered groups about them, who are not at all interested in doing so, but who have established contact with what they feel to be entities from other worlds and who have directed their lives according to the dictates of those Space Beings. Many of these men and women continue to work in conventional jobs, confiding their experiences only to close associates and, in some instances, developing psychic abilities which they utilize only for their families' and their close friends' benefits.

Daniel Fry established his Understanding Incorporated in 1955 as a means of better spreading the teachings of A-Lan, whom Fry claimed to have met on his first trip in a UFO. Fry remains active as a lecturer, and has directed one of the largest of the Flying Saucer Movement groups, containing over sixty units.

In 1955, George King was named the "Primary Terrestrial Mental Channel" by Master Aetherius of Venus. King has since been declared an agent of the Great White Brotherhood and a channel for both Aetherius and Master Jesus. Members of the Aetherius Society are earnestly engaged in the war being waged by the Brotherhood against the Black Magicians, a group they feel seeks to enslave the human race.

The Solar Light Center originated in 1965 in the Solar Cross Fellowship headed by Rudolph Pestalozzi, a channel for an entity named Baloran. The Solar Light Center itself was founded by Marianne Francis and Kenneth Keller, who worked together until the Light Center absorbed the Solar Cross Fellowship.

Miss Francis has been renamed Aleuti Francesca, and she most consistently channels for Sut-ko, the entity who originally revealed his messages to the Solar Cross organization. The Solar Light Center, through the lectures and works of Ms. Francesca, has also received contacts from Devas and other nature entities such as those involved with Findhorn Community in Scotland.

The Light Affiliates of British Columbia were headed by the late Mrs. Aileen Steil; she received her initial contact experience during the first week of April, 1969, when she saw a pink light in the sky over Burnaby, British Columbia, while walking her dog. She ran to the house to get her daughter Robin to come out and verify the mysterious aerial object. It was Robin who began to channel material, which led to the book *Aquarian Revelations* (1971).

There are two Space Brother groups functioning near Detroit. One is centered on the channeling of Baird Wallace, who began communicating with ''Kro'' of Neptune in 1956. Wallace's material was published in 1972 as *The Space Story and the Inner Light*.

A group headed by Warren H. Goetz has published a book called *The Intelligence of the Universe Speaks*. Goetz lives in Michigan's upper peninsula and claims to have seen his first UFO when he was but a child. He alleges to have taken many trips on flying saucers.

The Milwaukee, Wisconsin, area is the home of June (Bright Star) Young, principal channeler for the Arising Sun, who began receiving material in April 1971 when she had a vision involving the Archangel Michael.

In nearby Kiel, Wisconsin, Maxine Stoelting is one of the principal channelers for the Mu-Ne-Dowk Foundation. Maxine received her first telepathic message in April 1972 from a visiting family from Uranus, who purported to be living in the fourth dimension at the farthest end of a nearby lake.

Ancient Astronauts

Rev. Gordon Melton, Institute for the Study of American Religion, has observed that while the leaders of the Ancient Astronaut Society would undoubtedly deny its religious base, there seems to be little doubt that religion motivates that movement. Eric Von Daniken himself has stated that the theory came to him on an astral trip, and that he knows himself to be a reincarnated ancient astronaut.

"As with many psychic groups, little or no criticism of Von Daniken's hypothesis—necessary testing for a scientific hypothesis—is allowed," said Dr. Melton. "On the contrary, emphasis is placed on reviewing artifacts which might confirm the basic presupposition.

"In the flying-saucer literature, even with its divergences of ideas and emphasis, one sees an emerging, full-blown *Weltanschauung* theology and metaphysics. Such a perspective has been developed by a reference to the data channelled from the Space Brothers and speculations upon the UFO phenomena. The Ancient Astronauts represent the maturity of the movement, as they supply it with what in Christianity are church histories and scholarly technicians."

Children of the Gods

This is the way it was revealed to French journalist Claude Vorilhon on October 7, 1975, when he claimed to have an encounter with extraterrestrial beings, who brought him aboard their spacecraft.

Vorilhon learned that his hosts were the Elohim referred to in the creation story of Genesis, the "gods" who made man in their image. Elohim in Hebrew means "those who came from the sky," Vorilhon explained.

The primitive ancestors of modern man interpreted those strangers from the sky as "gods," because to them anyone arriving from the heavens could only be divine. It was the Elohim, who, as related in Genesis, created *Homo sapiens* in their image. Rather than some mystical act of creation, Vorilhon was informed that the Elohim structured humankind in their laboratories, utilizing deoxyribonucleic acid (DNA), just as our own contemporary Earth scientists are at the point of creating "synthetic" humans in the same process.

In a manner similar to Pygmalion creating a statue so beautiful that he fell in love with it, certain of the Elohim found the results of their laboratory artistry compellingly irresistible:

And it came to pass, when men began to multiply on the face of the earth, and daughters were born unto them, that . . . when the sons of God came in unto the daughters of men, and they bare children to them, the same became mighty men which were of old, men of renown. (Genesis 6:4)

The extraterrestrials told Vorilhon that the Elohim had sent great prophets, like Moses and Ezekiel, to guide humankind. Jesus, the fruit of a union between the Elohim and Mary, a daughter of man, was given the mission of making the Elohim's messages of guidance known throughout the world in anticipation of the Age of Apocalypse— which in the original Greek meant the "age of revelation," not the "end of the world." It is in this epoch, which we entered in 1945, that humankind will be able to understand scientifically that which the Elohim did aeons ago in the Genesis story.

The Space Beings explained to Vorilhon that, after the nuclear explosions in 1945, they believed that the Age of Apocalypse had arrived. The Elohim cannot return *en masse*, however, until the inhabitants of Earth display a greater ability to live together in fraternity and love. And they would like to see some evidence that the planet can be governed with intelligence and spirit before they fully reveal themselves to the planet at large.

Vorilhon says that the Elohim renamed him "Raels," which means "the man who brings light." He has since created the Raelian Movement, which reportedly counts over a thousand members in France. His appearances on radio and television are said to provoke thousands of telephone calls and letters.

Whether the year of 1945 did indeed precipitate accelerated cosmic concern with its violent displays of atomic power, or whether some as yet unperceived evolutionary mechanism was activated according to a timing device set in humankind's prehistory, large segments of our species seemed once again to become more receptive to the possibility of otherworldly visitations.

Welcome to the Fourth Dimension

According to the doctrines of the Space Beings, the most essential element in the overall hierarchal program is to lift humankind into the fourth dimension. The UFO contactees have been informed that the race of humans on Earth has been the laggard among the solar system. Due to the efforts of the Space Beings and their increased emphasis upon a mass educational program designed to help humankind evolve, the citizens of Earth will soon be able to rejoin the Federation of Planets. Once this has taken place, Earthlings will coordinate and cooperate with the brothers and sisters of other planes and planets.

A direct invitation to the Fourth Dimension was pronounced by the space entity OX-HO:

"There is a whole new world waiting for you people of Earth. The fourth dimension is one of subtleness, of lighter shades of beauty. With your increased vibrations you will be able to see this subtleness with an intensity beyond your imagination . . . the very earth on which you stand will be stepped up in frequency to match this dimensional vibration and each form of life will take on new shades of being.

"There are seven dimensions of being. Each planet understands one dimension at a time, but as we aid your evolution, your Earth will be stepped up in frequency and vibration to the next level. . . .

"Life is interdimensional, and so is man. . . . Learn to flow with these dimensional frequencies and learn to become flexible. Do not allow yourself to become crystallized, for each man has a shattering point if he continues to resist the flow of dimensional evolution. . . .

"People of Earth, you are becoming fourth dimensional whether you are ready or not. Leave the old to those who cling to the old. Don't let the New Age leave you behind."

The Space Beings have been patient, for they have been coming to Earth for many thousands of years, ever since they were rejected by humankind during the final days of Atlantis. Many of the Space Beings have even incarnated on Earth and have lived as Earthmen.

The Space Beings are doing all that they can to help humankind, but they cannot force themselves on us or take control of the conditions here, however bad things might be. It is a dictum of the Federation that visitors from other planets cannot interfere with our free will.

Contactees have been told that the Space Beings hope to guide Earth to a period of great unification, when all races will shun discriminatory separations and all of humankind will recognize its responsibility to every other life form existing on the planet. The Space Beings also seek to bring about a single, solidified government, which will conduct itself on spiritual principles and permit all of its citizens to grow constructively in love.

Representatives of a Spiritual Government

In order to achieve such a goal, the Hierarchal Board has established a program to help raise all men and women on Earth to higher consciousness. The teachings and the guidance of the Hierarchy is being beamed to Earthlings even as they lie in the sleep state.

Although the goal seems at times to be difficult to attain, the contactees have been informed that the Christ-self of each person on Earth is in full accord with the Hierarchal Board's program of increased awareness preparatory to the Second Coming of Christ Consciousness.

One of the major messages delivered by the Space Beings is that they come as representatives of a spiritual government: a hierarchy of intelligences seeking to elevate man's position in the universe and his awareness that he is an integral part of the Cosmos.

Certain of the Space Beings have told the contactees that they have come to Earth to give us the benefit of knowledge derived from their own suffering through aeons of time. They have evolved to the state beyond that which we presently are striving to achieve on Earth. They are well aware of the struggle of birth into this consciousness; but they promise that once it has been achieved, it is but the beginning. It is the start of life. They define life as the creative force flowing through all manifestations of God.

Today we are in the dark womb of Nativity called Earth. As we emerge from this womb to cry out into the new light of day, which the Space Brothers define as Christ consciousness, we will see that we have just begun to live, to grow, to understand, and to be in the Father-Mother Creator's home and being.

Powers and Principalities

It is of extreme importance to the UFO missionaries at this time to acquaint the people of Earth as dramatically as possible with the fact that they are not alone in the universe, that there are other planes and other planets in the solar system which bear intelligent life. The Space Beings feel that they must educate all planes revolving in and around the Earth to the fact that other living entities have experiences on planes and planets other than Earth.

The Space Beings look upon this as a solar system problem and one which requires a fully integrated, interdimensional, and interplanetary ruling. They say that the Hierarchal Board of the solar system evolves slowly, methodically, and enjoyably with thousands of rulers on many grades, who today participate in solar system government.

Those of us of Earth are but one consideration of the entire Hierarchal Board's plan and program. We must learn to appreciate our relationship to the rest of the solar system. The Space Beings have acknowledged that it will be many years before Earth will be in full knowledge of all things regarding the interplanetary board of the solar system.

According to the space entities, all planets are to come under the ruling of the Hierarchal Board. Once membership status is gained willingly, there is to be free exchange between worlds, such as that which exists between the states of the United States of America. Space Beings tell us through the contactees that it has taken 200,000 years for many planets in the solar system to approve of what is now coming to its final stage.

Solar Government

The space entity OX-HO defined solar government for the Light Affiliates:

"Solar government consists of many forms of spiritual justice which have been sent down by selected groups of beings who have been chosen for the specific task of enforcing God's laws of Oneness, balance, and Love.

"It is difficult to explain these laws to Earthlings for you have set concepts about law and order and individual ideas about right and wrong. The laws sent down to the Solar Councils of the various galaxies are universal. They include the balance of planets, the behavior patterns which the various planets emanate into the atmosphere, and the stabilization of the solar systems by enforcing certain rules.

"You people of Earth have broken the particular rules which combine the necessary requisites for outside help. There is a great cosmic law which says no other planetary culture may interrupt the evolution of another, for all civilizations have free will. But you Earthlings have entered into a way of doing that has upset the planets of your solar system. We cannot allow you to continue such action any longer. Therefore, we have called upon beings from the various galaxies to help you to help yourselves.

"We can see clearly that you are heading for destruction. . . . I'm afraid that we Space Brothers of the Confederation must step in before it is too late."

Structural Changes in Humans and the Planet Earth Are Now Taking Place

"Orlon" transmitting from the XY7 craft. Aleuti Francesca, channeler:

"I [communicate] on this specific occasion due to the

fact that there are certain basic, fundamental changes taking place within the structure of your planet.

"How does this relate between individuals on your planet and your planet itself?

"I will be more specific. You have already been told that the year of 1975 was a year of major change upon the planet Terra [Earth], and that the decisions made during this year would have far-reaching effects up to and beyond the year 2000 of your time.

"We are now stating that due to the high velocity waves reaching your planet from the Central Sun, imminent change or breakthrough in consciousness can occur at any time to any individual. We are speaking in terms of *sudden, abrupt changeover in consciousness or modes of thought, concepts, ideas*.

"At the same time, there are tremendous energies pouring in, in what you most probably would speak of as an ultraviolet radiation belt (that is the nearest we can describe in your language what is happening). Due to these energies, structural change within the molecular structure of the planet, the atoms of the physical planet, also can experience rapid or drastic switch-over patterns between stability and total instability. These could cause movements of land masses, air currents, and all manner of weather and related phenomena.

"We have already spoken to you of the imminence of much change of structural levels deep in the bowels of your planet. We now state to you that similar structural changes will be happening in individuals, causing, in many ways, sudden breakthrough into higher levels of consciousness—and in others, sudden breakthrough into total chaos or instability patterns.

"In the third phase of manifestation (in which you now find yourselves), both levels, or extremes of raising of consciousness and total chaotic consciousness, would manifest upon your planet. If you will observe, our brothers, our sisters, you will see both of these extremes now operating within your own experience and environs. Therefore, our communication upon this occasion deals specifically with the nature of the point of change within the individual, within the planet.

"*The point of change is within you,* and all individuals wishing to make major breakthroughs in consciousness are advised to use every means at their disposal, as this period will make simpler such adjustments and changeover in consciousness.

"There is a new pattern emerging for the future of your planet and for the future of New Age Man upon your planet."

Free Will

Channeled through Yolanda, Mark-Age:

"We never lose sight of the fact that man has free will. Man's will was given, is given, by the spiritual Source within us all in order that man may learn the one and only solution to all creation: To work in and through the Father-Mother Creative Principle called God.

"Until each man in every part of the universes has completed this understanding and mission, none of us are entirely free to evolve as a complete creation or race. We are bound together in one body, called mankind, throughout all the universes. We are cells within that body and are related to one another equally."

Transition, Rather than Apocalypse

The UFO contactees have been accused of belonging to the uncomfortable category of the "Doomsday Prophets." In actuality, those men and women who claim communication with Space Beings speak more often of a Time of Transition than of a Judgment Day. There is far more contactee channeling regarding the "raising of Earth's vibratory rate" than there are admonitions of repentance before the Apocalypse.

Perhaps, as some contactees have related, there have been many physical, group "Judgment Days." Each old age ends with a period of purgation which purifies those who survive the transitional period so that they might become better prepared for the emerging New Age.

According to several contactees, these periodic Judgment Days occur approximately every two thousand years. If this is so, then it truly is no coincidence that hundreds of men and women are now claiming contact with entities and intelligences in the same kind of spiritual unrest that characterized the Apostolic era.

Another two thousand years have run their course on some great Cosmic Calendar, and another transitional "Judgment Day" is at hand. It is once again time for young men and women to see visions, and old men and women to talk to God in their dreams. The transition from one age to another requires a higher level of consciousness than did existence in the previous epoch.

It may well be, then, that there is an internal consistency in the ageless messages of revelation that may at first lead one to consider that the Mind of God might really be some supercosmic transmitter that has endlessly broadcasted the same message to all of the world's saints, mystics, and other inspired men and women of history. But if the prophets of 3000 B.C., the apostles of 30 A.D., and the UFO contactees of 1980 have all been receiving essentially the same messages, then might we not conclude that the very repetition of a basic program of spiritual and physical survival may be evidence of the vital relevancy and the universality of certain cosmic truths?

The Space Beings' Basic Message

What constitutes the essential messages and admonitions received by the contactees? In *The Space Story and the Inner Light*, Baird Wallace states that the basic theme of the contact story is simple, but "its scope rocks much of the provincial thinking of people on Earth because of the glimpse it gives us into the incredible vistas of the worlds and life around us of which we have been, for the most part, unaware."

The Space Beings' visitation to our planet in this present period is for two primary reasons:

1. There has been grave concern about our indiscriminate use and experimentation with atomic energy, particularly in building instruments of war. The [Space Beings'] history shows that another planet in our solar system blew itself up with such devices by war between its people.

    This event, listed in our Bible [Exodus 7] during the time that the children of Israel were in Egypt, caused the rivers to turn to blood and the fish to die, due to the falling radioactive dust of a planet which once existed between Mars and Jupiter and which is now seen by our astronomers as the Asteroid Belt. Our Bible again refers to this event in Isaiah 4:12: "How art thou fallen from heaven, O Lucifer, Son of the morning?" The planet Lucifer (known to our Space Brothers as Maldek) was then the morning star of Earth.

    For the protection of our people and their people they have interfered with certain atomic experiments being conducted by both the United States and the USSR, which they indicate would have blown up the entire planet if carried out.

    The Space Brothers have pointed out that all of our experiments and uses of atomic energy are harmful to man and his world. The atmosphere and its protective electrical fields, which shield our planet from conditions of outer space, are particularly vulnerable to these energies. By using atomic energies, man is gradually destroying this protection, and outside influences, which will have dramatic impact on our weather and other natural conditions, will continually become more apparent as time passes.

2. The second and most important reason for the Space Brothers' visitation to Earth at this time is that our entire solar system is in transit into a new area of space, a new density, and that this is changing the vibratory rate of the nucleus of every atom in our planet, raising it to a higher frequency. They point out that all life on our planet, plant and animal and the consciousness of man, is also being affected by this new lifting in vibratory rate which is now upon us.

This change is particularly a problem for man of Earth because he has fallen behind in his spiritual evolution and is not ready for the events which are at hand. For this reason, our brothers from other worlds have emphasized that every man and woman on this planet must make a choice and that this choice is being presented to them in terms they understand regardless of their special condition of life.

Each and every one of us must decide within the depths of our consciousness, in terms which are real to us, whether we wish to give ourselves in service to our Creator and to our fellow man, or whether we wish to continue in the ways common to most Earth people and seek the service of ourselves.

Our brothers from space have stated that they have been sent by the will of our Infinite Creator to help those who choose the path of love and service to raise themselves to a new consciousness, the level of consciousness which, in not too many years, will be necessary for man if he would continue to live and evolve with this planet as it enters fully into the new area of space which will bring about the period many have called the New Age.

The Transition to Physical-Etheric

Aleuti Francesca, "telethought channeler" of the Solar Light Center, has relayed messages from entities who are concerned with people's ability to step up their personal frequency. According to "Voltra of Venus":

"You will still be yourselves; you will still function as human beings with all the sense perceptions of human beings. But you will be of a more rarefied construction. Transition from physical to fourth etheric substance will take place.

"Many of us with whom you speak are of this composition in our bodies and therein has lain much of the misunderstanding among your people as to our nature. We can and do lower the frequency rate of our bodies to become visible to the physical retina of your eyes. We are *physical-etheric*, whereas you are *physical-dense*.

"The composition of all matter on your planet is rapidly reaching a point wherein it will either become a finer etherialized structure or will disintegrate. . . .

"Our purpose at this time is to educate those of you who will work with us at and after the time of the frequency change. . . . We once more stress that you will not become . . . discarnate beings: you merely step up one level and gain so much by so doing. Your sense perceptions, rather than being eliminated, will only become heightened and an awareness of all that which is of beauty, of love, of eternal nature, will become as one with you. . . ."

6

An Invitation to Other Worlds

*S*emjase told Fred Bell that a trip from Earth to the Pleiades could take place in seven hours of our time. When we hear such an allegation, we most certainly wish to learn more about the Pleiadeans' method of overcoming time and space.

"When you go to the Pleiades in seven hours you are not overcoming time, you are overcoming space," Fred explained.

"The way their propulsion systems work, it is very simple. They merely go up into space, get outside of the planetary environment, take a 'picture' of where they are, then take a 'picture' of where they want to be. They have a picture already stored in the ship's computer of where they want to be, and the mechanism in the ship that recorded this picture of the universe above and below the ship where it is now, converts itself over from a camera to a projector. Then once it has digested the information of where it is, it projects the picture of where it wants to be.

"The time travel process is a converter that basically controls the amount of time it takes to assimilate the energy of the present location, and to disseminate the information of where it wants to be in order to project that information. This is what time travel is all about.

"The trip could appear to take place instantaneously. They don't need seven hours to get to the Pleiades. They could be there instantly.

"Take a cell in the body," Fred suggested by way of illustration, "and assume that this cell wants to transmit instantaneously the energy and intelligence in its essence from the head to the foot. Well, rather than get into the bloodstream and move slowly through the arteries, through the head, through the toes—throughout the entire body—it would be quicker to get into the human aura, which is moving much faster, and transmit from the auric frequencies of the base of the foot. You would have what would appear to be instantaneous travel, but what you've done is taken another corridor. Rather than go through the accepted corridor of the bloodstream of the body, you've now gone into the auric field, which is much faster and much more direct.

"It is the same thing with travelling across vast distances in our solar system," Fred went on. "The path of motion is what the astronomers are used to examining—the mechanical part, that is. Science looks at the mechanical outlay of the entire universe, but within the mechanical outlay of that universe is an energy field that has its own auric field. By moving about in that auric field, it's a lot easier to get from one place to another—and the speeds at which the auric fields move are pretty much instantaneous.

"These lines of the auric field can be calculated; they can be charted," Fred stated. "They *have been* calculated; they *have been* charted, and they have been made available to different races. They are something that is shared. The charts have information in them that is stored in their computers. They register locales of energy, which is what the Pleiadeans use to travel through space.''

The Pleiadean Beam Ships

A beam ship is a vehicle that transports people across interstellar distances in relatively short periods of time. Basically, it is sound-powered and light-powered. It projects a beam, it flies within this beam, and it warps space within this beam—as if it creates a scaler wave and then flies into it. But this is all done on a beaming principle. The energy is literally beamed out, which creates a void, and then the spaceship flies into the void. Once it's in a void, it beams again and flies to the next void, and so on. It does this in multiples of fours and eights. This is how the ships move faster than the speed of light from one place to another. The beam is not just a colorless, soundless beam; it has a very beautiful sound to it with a lot of colors. It's a very ecstatic thing to behold.

On February 26, 1980, Semjase explained more to Fred Bell about the beam ship.

''Its construct changes with each engineer, a male. His mate is the pilot, a female. The male is the power source. The female is the director of the power.

''Each ship lives only through a particular crew. When that crew dies, the ship also dies. The ships are the crew members' signatures of life purpose and comprise a karmic debt on their life span.

''The beam ship, in essence, is the creation of the captain and his soul mate. The crew members are on a journey to the Creator, and this is the only path for them. Someday they too will find their soul mates. To be a part of the beam ship construct is to embark on a life of purpose and dedication to service.

On November 14, 1981, Semjase added the following data concerning the beam ships:

"When the vehicles are once again constructed on Earth, as they have been in the past, the Federations will govern their purpose. The Council Elders know well the rules of the forces herein and esteem them as the wisdom of the ages.

"A proper relationship with the Forces is, of course, as important as a proper family relationship, being the root of the cause. Biological formations are expressions of these divine essences. The ancient Essenes procured their original doctorates by the natural laws that we are now sharing.

"Our beam ship technology cornerstones upon the four-square principle. As you grow more into this lifetime, I will share greater intellect with you and clarify many details that you do not yet understand."

Control of a Pleiadean Ship

"Control of a Pleiadean ship is done mentally and physically," Fred Bell stated. "I have been able to control one of their ships from the ground, using different grid systems that I've developed.

"Once in New Mexico I had the grid systems in a motor home. I was able to use the grids to enhance thought forms that were being sent directly into the master computer of the ship. The Pleiadean technology is such that certain unblocked thought forms are run through their filters. If you can penetrate their filter system, you can control their computer, which then, in turn, controls their ship."

In this particular instance in New Mexico, Semjase brought down some of the blocks and made it easier for Fred to access the computer so that he was able mentally to direct the ship.

"It isn't just a matter of thinking the thought," he

continued. "You have to have a certain abridgement of thought forms. You have to have a certain awareness of how to access the computer. You have to have a certain idea of how the computer works and the proper sequencing of thoughts to make it perform. Otherwise, it will just negate anything that's coming into it.

"I was able to override certain barriers. Even though Semjase had dropped the main barrier, I was still able to override certain things and cause the ship to perform in certain ways. Basically, what it did is that it came straight down through some clouds where it was invisible to a low altitude, to a point where it was visible. It made a left-hand turn above the horizon and disappeared across Interstate 10."

Semjase's Home Planet Erra

The terrain of Erra resembles the Swiss Alps. It does have some flatlands on it, but it is greener. The atmosphere is greener in color because of the density of the various gases on the planet—and because it has a second sun that is slightly visible. Although the second sun is not very bright, not greatly apparent, it is there.

The vegetation on Erra is very similar to ours, but it is more highly advanced due to the fact that it hasn't been impeded over generations by pollution. They do no mining on that planet. They don't do anything to harm the soil, so it's much more harmonious than on Earth.

One of the interesting things Fred Bell has been told about Erra is in regard to its flowers. In order to get the maximum benefit of the sun, some of the flowers change color throughout the periods of the day. They might be a violet shade in the morning and a reddish hue at night, so they can absorb the opposite of the spectrum of the sun as it moves through the day. This process gives the flowers much more vitality.

The Pleiadeans have horticulture as a hobby because they believe that working with plants keeps them closer to God. And because horticulture keeps them closer to God, it keeps them more grounded.

Their genetic research is quite a bit more advanced than ours. They grow plants to a certain point, freeze-dry them without having them shrivel, then coat them with a substance that makes them hard as steel.

The Pleiadeans are aware of those plants that trap light and color and sound energies and then release them into the human consciousness. Although they are not into "getting high," their foods are more elevated.

The general environment of Semjase's planet is rather quiet. They don't have sirens and fire engines and all the kinds of noise pollution that we do.

Their structures are built into the sides of mountains, and they are very harmonious with the topography. The buildings that they live in are oftentimes of quartz or a highly refined glass that refracts light in different rainbow patterns. Erra is a bit more colorful than we know life here on Earth.

The Invitation to Intergalactic Citizenship

Semjase seems eager to convince Fred Bell and, in turn, all of humankind, that the Pleiadeans do not consider themselves superior as a species to Earthlings. They have come to help guide us through the transitional period known as "the Last Days." Man, they emphasize, is a citizen of the universe. He is not isolated on this planet, but he must evolve to a higher stage of awareness so that he might become a contributing member to a larger community of intelligence.

It is as if the space intelligences have been given an assignment to help direct their younger brothers and sisters to a higher level of spirituality.

The contactees, understandably, become quite impatient from time to time and ask their extraterrestrial mentors why they do not accelerate the program.

Why do they not automatically make man a citizen with full right of franchise in the Cosmos?

Why do these Space Brothers not reveal themselves *en masse* to Earth people to convince those who are skeptical, to startle those who are apathetic?

Why do they not demonstrate, once and for all, that there is an intelligence outside of men and women who does care and who is steadily interacting with them? Surely certain orthodox church members could make the transition from angel to Space Being.

The space entities answer that they are holding Earth together with their beams of energy. They have told such channelers as Mark-Age that too many things have to be demonstrated on Earth before such a mass landing or mass revelation of the Space Beings can take place.

The extraterrestrials' current rationale is that mass Earth consciousness will have to accept and to desire an interplanetary and, eventually, an interdimensional council, before any representative from the Earth plane can be taken out of the atmosphere—or for that matter, before any member of the extraterrestrials can descend upon planet Earth. The space entities assure the contactees that this is not a matter of individual preference and understanding. It is a planetary question.

The space intelligences have declared that they will not overrule the mass desire.

"Please understand this basic rule of the universal law," stated a space intelligence through a UFO channeler at Mark-Age. "Don't expect us to come down and force you into seeing us or accepting us. This must be accomplished from the Earth plane level. Please understand.

"We love you so. We love you individually. We love the Earth as a planet, and as a place in the solar system, as we understand each planet as a part of the body of this solar system.

"We cannot love one part of the solar system more than another. We cannot come in and force or command it. It must come from the desire to be at-one-ment with the rest of the solar system.

"We love you, those who are instruments. You are representatives and ambassadors from our levels and planets. We protect, and teach, and guide you, because you are one of us. You have volunteered for your missions. We have volunteered for ours.

All Who Desire Communication May Receive It

For those who ask if they might be permitted to receive direct communication from the Space Brothers, a space entity once responded to such a question at a Mark-Age function by stating:

"If you desire this, you may have it. All are capable of direct communication. You merely have to ask, then be receptive. We do not set the time. We work through your teachers. Your own teachers and spiritual aides and guides will let us know when we can come through.

"Of course, remember, too, spiritual guides and teachers are your own Christ-aware self, as well as those who are assigned to help your development.

"We are here only as assistants to your own individual teachers. We are not your teachers in this particular program. It is not our mission. We are here as supplementary aides from other planets, dimensions, and galaxies for purposes yet beyond your knowledge and need to coordinate. We have a function that will not be portrayed to you for many years. In the meantime, we work in this intunement in communication level.''

In another Mark-Age channeling session, the space intelligence contact gave interesting details as to the makeup of not only the extraterrestrials, but of the program of interaction with humankind.

The entity speaking through the channel on that occasion said that each of the space entities has a different specialization. They work and are drawn together by spirit and by the teachers that control and influence their experiences and developments. They were brought together to complement and to supplement each other's talents and specializations. They were brought from many realms and dimensions and planets.

The extraterrestrial said that even their spacecraft was an experiment in time and space, just as the life of each man is an experiment in the experience of God, the Father-Mother Creator; just as the planet is an experiment to see how a particular grouping and congregation of spiritual energies will work together.

''We understand these things,'' the entity said. ''Sometimes we find it necessary for one to be removed or another to be brought in. We are not static. We do not have set ideas of what we are and what we must manifest. We work by tuning in to the spiritual force within us and the spiritual force which is created by the group brought together.

''Each one is assigned, in a sense, to a certain individual upon the Earth planet at this time. We are alerted by the various methods we have of mind control in electronics and magnetic equipment—terms which we use for your convenience which really do not explain our equipment—and through these means, we know your present development.

''We are in communication through our High-Self activities with the High-Self spirit within you. We read your auras.

"We know what your spiritual evolvement is. We know through communication with your own High-Self consciousness what is best for you at a particular time. We bow only to the law within you.

"We are the guiding influences in your life. We are purposely set up to see an overall global picture of the western hemisphere."

The Change in Global Consciousness

The space intelligences have often told the contactees that while humans have higher dimensional bodies, they cannot be lifted outside their own atmosphere at this time without severely affecting what is to take place on higher realms and at the outer fringes of space. The contactees have been reassured that there is a change in consciousness for every man, woman, and child on planet Earth. None will be excepted.

The space entities have also expressed their dismay that not all of their contactees are willing to speak forth. Not all are even conscious of what they are receiving in dreams and in meditations and in contacts with fellow beings from other worlds and other dimensions. But they emphasize that each man and woman is given the opportunity for making such judgments and conditions in his or her own thinking patterns.

The Space Brothers emphasize repeatedly that cosmic truth reveals that all humans have been many things and are related to all life, all creative forces.

The extraterrestrials state that they have come not only to give us information, but to bestow love upon us. Love is a force, they tell us, just as thought is a force. They bring us this force to take from us and to give to us, so that they can open up the flow in the whole solar system.

Interestingly, the space entities often stress that the thoughts of humankind are able to reach out and somehow affect the solar system and beyond. It is because, they say, we are a part of God, they are a part of God, and all beings are interrelated.

The Interdependence Between /pace Being and Human

The Space Beings also give expression to an interdependence that seems to exist between them and humankind. In a Mark-Age channeling, an entity once related:

"Therefore, what you *think* affects us, and it's time you began to realize it! We realize that what we think affects you and that what you think affects you. So our purpose is twofold:

"We come to teach you how to think for your own evolvement and we come to achieve further our own evolvement. In this way, we are interrelated.

"If you do not think healthy thoughts, progressive thoughts, evolutionary thoughts for your own good, then we cannot fully grow, either. We control greatly our own lives and planets, but we are affected by the mass consciousness of this particular planet; and you are involved in that mass consciousness because you contribute to it.

"We ask you, then, to give forth holy thoughts. The word holy in your language means 'whole,' which is God. God is holy and God is whole. Spirit is unseparated. We ask you to reach us with your thoughts, as we can reach you with our thoughts.

"We are demonstrating this, for instance, through a channel. We make contact in a mental way. Mind to mind, stimulating various brain centers, so certain ideas, never thought of or unfrequently accepted, become part of the consciousness. We can come into the spiritual aura at any time, any place; for in spirit, all is one; all is good; for good is God. And there we are united forever and never can change.''

Achieving Mastery of Higher Consciousness

"The Pleiadean ships do move through the etheric planes," Fred Bell agreed, "but understand that the etheric is a part of the physical world, as are we. It is just that we have not yet realized our true potential on these planes.

"You remember when Jesus was here and people tried to stone him? He became invisible, and the crowd wondered what manner of man he was that he could disappear among them.

"Part of what Jesus taught is that we all have the ability to move up in the etheric levels. Normally our bodies are physically dense because of what we eat and how we behave, so it is pretty hard to move up to the etheric.

"The Pleiadeans are a lot less physically dense than we are. If you touched one of them, however, they would feel much the same as we do. It is just that they are less physical and have attained a much greater control over their emotions.

"If you can learn to combine your mind and your emotional body, your astral body, together, you can do tremendous things with your physical body.

"I am not saying that all Pleiadeans have this kind of control. I've only met a few of them," Fred stated.

"There is a very human side to them," he continued. "They have their differences, their arguments. But they have the ability to blend together quite rapidly in their group feeling and to move upward to the etheric planes."

As far as their becoming invisible, they appear to have devices which assist them in attaining such a state. Fred believes that he can re-create a lot of their technology, and he is working on such a device right now.

When more of us reach the level of consciousness that is common among the Pleiadeans, so many of those apparent miracles that we now call "super feats" will become possible.

"I am convinced that our children's children will be able to levitate at will, for example, as well as attain an invisible state. I think the human race is fast approaching these abilities," Fred commented.

7

Amazing Energies from the Pleiades

Fred Bell is convinced that his work with the antipollution devices, which he claims were given to him by Semjase, fit in with the Big Picture of extraterrestrial contact.

"The pollution work that I do and the lecturing that I do all over the world—the television shows, the radio shows and things like that that I've done for over fifteen years—are very important toward changing the environment of this planet," he explained.

"Semjase pointed out back in the seventies that this activity was going to be very necessary, and she showed me some of the things that weren't included in the *Global 2000* report or in some of my own studies. The environment is the first thing that has to be cleaned up, because the pollution in the biosphere is causing pollution in the mind."

When Semjase gave Fred the idea for the Pyradyne receptor,[1] which was back in about 1976, she was teaching

---

[1]According to Fred Bell, the Pyradyne Receptor, worn as a medallion, allows any given individual to experience changing external environmental conditions with a new clairvoyant view of the cause of the change as it occurs.

him about gene conditioning. "We're applying her teachings in our life-extension work," he said. "We're working with a sophisticated exchange in which the genes regulate the cells and the cell, in turn, regulates the regeneration and disintegration of the life form. The receptor modifies the DNA frequencies to the point where they begin to create new hormones in the body, thus manifesting higher and higher expressions of energy.

"All energy expressions, as we know them in our physical body, come from the secretion of hormones. The hormones arrive at the receptor site on the brain for a given period of time. While the receptor sites are being energized or de-energized on the brain pattern, the consciousness moves up the astral, etheric, and mental planes. This increased energy then regulates time, and when you regulate your own time slightly out of dimension with the Earth time, it separates you from the masses and gives you a very powerful form of individual creativity."

A Second Christmas Present from Semjase

Fred's second Christmas present from Semjase in 1981 was the development of a unit that he uses in his pyramid structures, and which alters time slightly in consciousness when one steps in front of it.

"When you accelerate the carbon atom in hyperspeeds or beyond the speed of light, what happens is, first of all, the carbon atom is represented as an octahedron—a pyramid with a pyramid top and a pyramid bottom," he said. "When you accelerate the carbon atom in the body faster than the speed of light, the actual form collapses. As it goes toward the speed of light, it gets smaller, as viewed from here on Earth, but it also changes form.

"You have to imagine, if you will, that the pyramid

'squashes' on itself. In other words, the top pyramid falls inside of the bottom pyramid; the bottom pyramid falls inside of the top one. It forms a Star of David. It also interpenetrates its own shape."

In Fred Bell's opinion, this is where the symbology of the Star of David came from originally. In the Jewish culture it represented the transcendental consciousness of the nation, but it also came from a scientific term, because at one time science and religion were one.

"What happens," Fred said, "is when this thing collapses toward the speed of light inside itself, in four quadrants, in each of the four corners of this structure are formed two pyramids inverted, so eight more pyramids will form out of subatomic material in this particular geometric shape. The design of this represents the cubit, because on the great pyramid there are four cornerstones around each pyramid. On the big pyramid there are four major cornerstones on which the whole structure is centered and aligned."

Interdimensional Flight

Semjase has told Fred Bell that in interdimensional flight the device collapses, and then as each succeeding dimension is attained, one of those four corners suddenly becomes the same structure as the original form. It's like cosmic mitosis; and this structure, as it goes into the next dimension, collapses on itself in one of the four corners. Then it continues to accelerate, replicating itself, each replication smaller than the previous one.

Theoretically, when the Pleiadean ships accelerate in hyperspeed, they are reduced down to energy. They finally reach a point of almost pure energy, and that's how they attain these really incredible speeds across the universe in a matter of microseconds.

Semjase once told Fred that their craft are sound-powered and light-separated when they attain the speed of light.

Analyzing Pleiadean Harmonics

As soon as the Pleiadean spacecraft start to move, Fred stated, the sound can no longer escape because of the compression of the force field around it. The faster they move, the quieter they become.

"We've had spectrum analyzers check out all of the different frequencies, and we now know each one. They use twelve different frequencies which blend into one frequency," Fred explained.

"First of all, there was a 4.9 cycle pattern, then there was a 4.6 cycle pattern and a 5.0 cycle pattern.

"Nicola Tesla discovered the natural electromagnetic resonance of Earth to be 6.6 cycles per second. Another researcher by the name of Schumann found a second resonance of the Earth of 7.8 cycles per second. These are all natural resonances. It is interesting that the Pleiadean ships run on these resonances."

When tapes of Pleiadean craft were further examined with a spectrum analyzer, technicians found a 7.14 cycle harmonic, a 4.72 harmonic, and a 3.52 cycle harmonic. There were twelve different harmonics, and there was a 1 kHz tone that existed throughout each wave and aligned all the other ones together. It appeared to be the master frequency that kept all of the other ones in harmony.

It appears that the Pleiadeans use a 1 kHz signal, 1000-cycles-per-second vibration, to stabilize these low-frequency sounds.

Semjase has told Fred Bell that the larger spaceship landing ports on Erra have buildings which are acoustically designed so that the reflection of the sound waves of the ships coming off the walls becomes a musical sound.

"Here in Los Angeles, if you go to LAX and watch a jetliner take off, it destroys your eardrums!" Fred laughed, shaking his head.

"Flight in one of their ships is like a psychedelic color ride. It's incredible just being in one of these things. I personally have never ridden in one, but Semjase has described the experience to me."

When Michael Pender of the Moody Blues heard a Pleiadean spacecraft in Hawaii, he created what he believed to be a very good duplication of it for one of his albums. (Fred thinks it was *Every Good Boy Deserves Favor*.) Pender did his version of the sound by way of a synthesizer, which got the feeling. He is considered to be a superior keyboard player, and he is probably one of the few people who could make a somewhat accurate representation of the actual sound of one of these things.

Fred received a recording of Semjase's spacecraft when Billy Meier and he were working together through Colonel Wendelle Stevens. Semjase told him that he must get the recording, because at that time he was working on the Time Machine. She said that he needed to get a feeling for the propulsion system.

Fred made a trip to Arizona and explained to Colonel Stevens why he needed the recording. Stevens felt that he had a right to know it, so he gave him a copy.

On that recording there is not only the sound of Semjase's ship, but also the sound of the Renticulum ships. The Renticulums, by the way, were the ones who were involved in the famous Betty and Barney Hill abduction case in New Hampshire in 1961.

"When I built the Time Machine two years ago, Semjase explained how they used time in relationship to space. She said, 'You must understand time before you work with space, because if you got lost in space and time, you would have a tremendous problem finding your way back.' "

In their propulsion systems, the Pleiadeans have two large rings of magnetic fluids held in suspension. These fluids pump in two different directions. Allen Holt, who Fred likes to call "the new Wernher von Braun of space," is working at NASA in charge of propulsion systems, primarily with Sky Lab and some of the projects in which the craft are going up and re-entering. Holt wrote a report that was sponsored by the American Institute of Aeronautics and Astronautics, the Society of Automotive Engineers, and the American Society of Mechanical Engineers, entitled "Prospects for a Breakthrough in Fuel Dependent Propulsion." This report was presented in a joint propulsion conference in 1980 in Hartford, Connecticut, and it comprises a crude outline of a system similar to that which is used in the Pleiadean ships.

Primarily, the Pleiadeans are using a superconducting magnet; and according to Fred Bell's explanation, "Imagine that you have twelve lasers in the center of a circle, each one pointing a beam out to an outer rim, so it would look like a wagon wheel—only instead of the hub in the wagon wheel, there would be twelve spokes, each one a laser beam. Around each spoke is a superconducting magnet, and the spokes themselves are hydromagnetic electron wave generators.

"The outer structure is the ring, and it has two fluids in it—one going in one direction, and one going in the other. This particular wheel is like the dual wheels on a truck— one has fluid in it that goes clockwise, one has fluid in it that goes counter-clockwise.

"These fluids have magnetic properties suspended in them. Special pumps begin to rotate them in opposite directions at a high rate of speed, which, first of all, gives them a gyroscopic effect. When the lasers come on, the plasma is pinched down and sent out through superconducting magnets. The focused plasma magnetically energizes the fluids in the outer rims, which are travelling at a fairly good rate of speed.

"Next, superconducting magnets begin to produce cyclic waves in the outer parameter of the two disks, and these cyclic waves begin to move in a clockwise and a counter-clockwise direction. They call them travelling waves.

"You can imagine this third clockwise wave travelling around inside these two different tires in the opposite direction. They will actually begin to warp the gravity around them and the space around them, and they begin to create gravity-like waves that are different from those on Earth. Pretty soon the craft does not see the Earth anymore, and it begins to lift itself off.

"We have in our country today the basic idea of such technology. The way the Pleiadeans travel is far more sophisticated, but we have begun to stretch our science."

Centering on Truth

One of the things about which Semjase used to chide Fred was the fact that he would always try to imagine more from their conversations and from what she was trying to teach him than was actually there. She constantly used to insist that if he would just stop using his imagination and just feel the truth of their communication, he would receive greater rewards.

"Semjase began to teach me that centering on truth actually exceeds the expectations of imagination, and that's how I've been able to take what, in the beginning, was a series of very abstract demonstrations and develop them into a science in which today I feel that I've been successful," he said. "Some of the scientific things that I was able to do years ago, I now see other New Age people doing. Not just a few hundred experimenters, but literally thousands of them. Every conversation I ever had with her is recorded in my notes. You must understand that when Semjase speaks to me, she is so intense that an entire book could be written about what she can say in a paragraph. If we are talking about the spaceships, if we are talking about relativity, it's so intense that I usually can only talk to her for maybe six minutes, seven at the most, and then she loses me. I get lost, I just can't deal with it anymore, because she goes right over my head.''

The Pleiadean Continuum

''The Pleiadeans are slightly out of dimension to us,'' Fred commented. ''It's a continuum. It's like a harmonic—the first harmonic of our continuum. Their normal vibration is slightly more subtle than it is here, but it is very easy for them to become physically apparent. An idea of a more subtle vibration would be like the etheric body as opposed to the physical body.

''Because we are so tuned to other things, the ways of man, we're not so aware of the Pleiadeans. It's very easy for them to become invisible.

''Invisibility is nothing more than moving up in vibration slightly beyond the center scale frequencies that the human eye is normally perceiving.

''The Pleiadeans are a bit higher in frequency, but they're from the same time reference that we are.''

8

The Atlantis Connection and Our Extraterrestrial Ancestors

The Space Being OX-HO on America and the Karma of Atlantis:

"America right now is feeling the effect of the Karmic pattern of the Atlantean culture. Your young people are Atlanteans reborn to once again work out their Karma. They are filled to overflowing with the knowledge of the great civilization of Atlantis. Their arts and their scientific technology is greater than ever before, and you will begin to see this more and more distinctly.

"These young people want peace instead of war. That is their only wish this incarnation, for terrible destruction was visited upon them when they went in the land of Atlantis. Now their souls have evolved to a plateau wherein they seek only peace.

"Help the young to create harmony and peace, for they want it so desperately."

Dr. Fred Bell is convinced that a lot of the equipment

that he has developed today is based on the technology that he learned in a past life in Atlantis.

Many psychics have told him that he was one of the leading scientists in Atlantis during the time of its fall. A great deal of his technology was misused by the dark priests and was utilized to bring about the destruction of Atlantis. He has been held responsible for that in many, many different channelings.

"I accept this because technology, if it is misused, will destroy. Like the thermonuclear bombs that have been developed today—if they are misused, they are going to destroy us. If they're used peacefully, they can give us energy. I don't take responsibility for the human race in its misapplication, but I do take responsibility for advocating these inventions."

Contactees who combine Atlantean lore and UFOlogy have created several fascinating scenarios regarding visitations in ancient times by beings from another world.

Some of these men and women ask us to consider the probability that superior alien beings visited the earth in antediluvian times. These aliens may have pointed to the skies and remarked that they came from a planet in our own galaxy or some other cluster of stars. These UFOlogists may have described "home" as a utopian civilization with superior technology.

Such stories would have been spread by word of mouth, through priestly castes and wandering minstrels. Perhaps, to lend additional credence to the tale, narrators may have changed the location of the utopia to a lost continent on our own planet.

One popular theory has it that, in some dim epoch of history, Atlantis was a supercivilization on earth that was endangered by an impending catastrophe—the advent of an ice age, earthquakes, the gradual shifting of the polar regions, or nuclear war. Whatever the danger, the technologically advanced country attempted to send colonists to another planet, and a few thousand survivors found an Earthlike planet in outer space.

Eventually, according to this theory, there was a longing for the planet of birth. In time, the Atlanteans sent back scout ships to Earth. They discovered that a few humans had survived the Atlantean disaster, but they were living as primitive cavemen with no knowledge of the grandeur that had been Atlantis. The returning astronauts counseled humanity in the arts of agriculture, law, religion, and social structure, and told their struggling cousins wondrous tales of the lost Atlantis.

Under this hypothesis, our modern world is a product of Atlantean knowledge and technology.

Ancient Aircraft

Ancient texts mention flying machines, advanced technology, and awesome weapons wielded by the gods.

The sacred Hindu hymns, the *Rig-Veda*, constitute some of the oldest known religious documents. The splendid poetry tells of the achievements of the Hindu gods, and one passage tells of Indra, a god-being, who was honored when his name was turned into "India."

Indra, who became known as the "fort-destroyer" because of his exploits in war, was said to travel through the skies in a flying machine, the *Vimana*. This craft was allegedly equipped with awesome weapons capable of destroying a city. Their effect seems to have been like that of a laser beam, or a nuclear device.

Another ancient Indian text, the *Mahabharata*, tells of an attack on an enemy army:

It was as if the elements had been unfurled. The sun spun around in the heavens. The world shuddered in fever, scorched by the terrible heat of this weapon.

Elephants burst into flames. . . . The rivers boiled.
Animals crumpled to the ground and died. The armies
of the enemy were mowed down when the raging of the
elements reached them. Forests collapsed in splintered
rows. Horses and chariots were burned up. . . . The
corpses of the fallen were mutilated by the terrible heat
so that they looked other than human. . . . Never before
had we heard of such a ghastly weapon.

Dare we believe that the legends and myths of our
ancestors are based on fact? If so, we may discover that
humanity's written history is in dire need of revision.
Ancient manuscripts are crammed with numerous accounts
of sky disks, flying chariots, cloud ships, and aerial
demons.

The Sky People

An example of such visits allegedly occurred in A.D. 840
when farmers, peasants, and tradesmen in Europe were
forbidden to barter with the "sky people."

Argobard, the Archbishop of Lyons, was visibly upset
because his parishioners believed in "ships from the clouds."
The aerial ships were supposedly piloted by beings of
normal, humanlike appearance from the "land beyond the
clouds . . . Magonia."

The occupants of the ships were certainly not supernatural beings. They traded artifacts and coins to French peasants for earthly fruits and vegetables.

In Contra Insulem Vivgi Opinionem, Archbishop Argobard
reported on the capture of a crew from one of the Magonian
flying machines.

"A certain assembly exhibited several people as cap-
tives," he wrote. "Three men and one woman, as if they
had fallen from the ships themselves. They had been de-
tained for some days in chains, then finally put on show to

the mob, and as I have said, in our presence they were stoned to death. . . .''

Such incidents undoubtedly led the "sky people" to use elaborate security measures when they next landed on Earth.

Throughout the dim corridors of history, we can find frequent mention of the legendary "sky people." Often these beings are considered to have been emissaries of the "flying serpent." The snake-worshipping Aztecs and Mayans are not far removed from the Chinese cultists, who worshipped a celestial dragon. Both races may have been contacted by emissaries from another planet.

The Star Gods Create Sumer

According to the historians, seven thousand years ago our ancestors suddenly decided to establish the Sumerian civilization. Until then, man had clubbed and fought his way through a primitive world. Overnight, the nomads and hunters created a miraculous city-state in the Mesopotamian valley—the beginning of our present civilization. With little effort, these primitive tradesmen left their tents and caves and became skilled in the arts of civilized living. They constructed homes, temples, towers, churches, and pyramids. They left the risky rewards of hunting and became farmers, tending the soil and irrigating the land. They became experts in the use of metals and ceramics, and in hundreds of other skills.

The Sumerians created a form of cuneiform writing. They built observatories for their astronomers and studied the stars. Their astronomers were so accurate that their measurements on the rotation of the moon deviate only 0.4 from the modern computerized figures. At the height of the ancient Greek civilization, the highest known number was 10,000. After that sum, the Greeks could only fall back on "infinity." The Sumerians were master mathematicians, and a tablet found on the Kuyunjik hills a few years ago contained a fifteen-digit number—195,955,200,000,000.

The Sumerian astronomers charted the stars as accurately as do our modern scientists. One pictograph depicts the planets revolving around the sun—something that Copernicus and Kepler postulated only five hundred years ago. Other Sumerian drawings show humanlike beings with helmets of stars. Other figures are drawn zooming through the skies on celestial, starred disks, or spheres.

Historians have a habit of dismissing legends about the origin of civilizations and nations, and they have discarded the Sumerians' own account of how their remarkable city-state was established.

A Babylonian priest and historian, Berosus, declared that the Sumerians once "lived like beasts in the field with no order or rule." The Sumerians lived exactly like their primitive forefathers until a bizarre "beast with reason" appeared in their midst, according to Berosus.

The gifted entity was endowed with a superior intelligence, but its appearance was frightening to behold. An amphibian, the "Oannes" had the body of a fish, humanlike feet on the end of a fish tail, and both a fish head and a human head.

Berosus explained that this fantastic fish-man walked about on land and counseled the ancient Sumerians, but that he returned to the ocean each evening.

"This being in daytime used to converse with the people," Berosus wrote. "But, it took no food at that season; and he gave them insight into letters and sciences and every kind of art. He taught them to construct homes, to found temples, to compile laws, and explained to them the principles of geometrical knowledge. He made them distinguish the seeds of the earth, and showed them how to collect fruits. In short, he instructed them in everything which could tend to soften the manners and humanize mankind.''

Let us assume that you are an extraterrestrial sent to Earth to instruct the primitive inhabitants on the rudiments of civilization. Let us also presume that *Homo sapiens* was seeded there many generations ago; it is now time to pass along knowledge from the mother planet. You will need a safe, secure headquarters for your crewmen and the spaceship, which is capable of underwater propulsion. Wouldn't you consider submerging your craft in a quiet lagoon and emerging on land each morning in an underwater diving suit? If we allow our imagination to expand we can see ancient scribes attempting to describe what is today a conventional diving suit, ''both a fish head and a human head.''

Legend/ of the /ky People

Legends of the Eskimos of the far north tell of how their ancestors were flown to the polar regions by god-like beings with metallic wings.

Farther south, we discover a Mayan tale of a gigantic metallic eagle landing from the heavens with ''the roar of a lion.'' The ''beak'' of the ''eagle'' opened and ''. . . four creatures, strange to our tribe, who did not breathe the air we breathe, walked from the marvelous eagle.''

The mythology of Peru says that the inhabitants of that area were born on Earth from silver, bronze, and golden eggs ''which floated down from the heavens.''

The *Popul Vuh*, which is the bible of the Quiches tribes in Guatemala, outlines another Mayan legend concerning visitors from the skies. These unusual beings possessed and used the compass. They knew the world was round. The *Popul Vuh* also related that these sky people knew the secrets of the universe, and that when the Quiches tribesmen became determined to steal these secrets, the visitors fogged their minds.

Were these unusual sky people the survivors of the Atlantean disaster or were they from another planet?

Homo sapiens views the universe through a slender speck of the visual spectrum, between 254 millimicrons on the one side to 2,400 on the other. We are looking out of our own world through a tiny crack and, perhaps arrogantly, proclaiming the dimensions of being. The traditional historical accounts are equally limited in their view of the past; few records exist of prior civilizations. Humankind's past is hidden in a mist of secrets, misunderstandings, and contradictions.

Children of the Divine Universal Power

The great metaphysician Rudolf Steiner theorized that the people of our prehistory (the Atlanteans) had been largely guided and directed by a higher order of beings who interacted and communicated with certain humans—the smartest, the strongest, the most intellectually flexible. Eventually, these select humans produced what might be called demigods, divine human beings who, in turn, could relay instructions from higher intelligences.

In effect, Steiner may have given us another definition of the progeny that the ancient Hebrews named "Nephilim," which does, in fact, mean demigods, men of "great renown."

Steiner went on to speculate that within the larger evolving human race were the descendents of those divine-human hybrid beings, men and women who are animated by higher ideals, who regard themselves as children of a divine universal power. It need not be overemphasized that the larger body of humankind is devoted to the service of egotism, materialism, and selfish personal interests.

Steiner believes that within what he termed the emerging "Sixth Post-Atlantean Race" would be children of the divine universal power who would be able to initiate those men and women who have developed their faculty of thought so that they might better unite themselves with the divine. The children of the divine universal power, those who have the "seed" within them, will be able to initiate the more advanced members of humankind, according to Steiner. People so initiated will be able to receive revelations and to perform what others will consider miracles. The initiates will go on to become the mediators between humankind and the higher intelligences.

The whole point of the efforts of these higher intelligences is to enable humankind to become more independent, more able to stand on its own feet without having to rely on the higher order of beings that directed humans in ancient times.

9

Egypt, the Titans, and Raiders of the Lost UFOs

Fred Bell believes that the life experience prior to his present one was as a German-Jewish archaeologist who was killed by the Nazis in an act of rivalry over artifacts of an extraterrestrial origin. Although the skeptical may suggest that that particular scenario is reminiscent of Steven Spielberg's *Raiders of the Lost Ark,* an increasing amount of evidence exists that reveals there is a great deal of truth both to Spielberg's fantasy and to Bell's alleged past life recall.

It can now be demonstrated that Hitler was exceedingly interested in secret societies, arcane wisdom, and mystical legends; and that he did indeed believe that such powerful spiritual artifacts as the Ark of the Covenant, the Spear of the Crucifixion, and the Holy Grail could make his Nazi party invincible. The Fuehrer also was quite convinced that representatives of alien cultures walked the Earth in secret and that it was his mission to create a master race who would be ready to interact and to interbreed with them.

And there may even be some truth to the allegation that the Nazis sought a spaceship in ancient Egypt that could serve as a prototype for a more effective jet engine and rocket ship than the ones over which their scientists already labored.

Hitler's Secret Quest

In April 1942, Nazi Germany sent out an expedition composed of its most visionary scientists to seek a military vantage point in the "Hollow Earth." Although the safari of leading scientists left at a time when the Third Reich was putting maximum effort in its drive against the Allies, Goering, Himmler, and Hitler enthusiastically endorsed the project. The Fuehrer had long been convinced that the Earth was concave and that man lived on the *inside* of the globe.

According to the theory advanced by the Nazi scientists, if the Third Reich were to position its most astute radar experts in the proper geometric area they would be able to determine the position of the British Fleet and the Allied bomber squadrons, because the concave curvature of the globe would enable infrared rays to accomplish long-distance monitoring.

When the Nazi exponents of the Hollow Earth hypothesis sent the expedition to the island of Rugen, they had complete confidence in their pseudoscientific vision. Those nearest the Fuehrer shared his belief that such a *coup* as discovering the entrance to the Inner World would convince the Masters who lived there that the Nazis were truly deserving of mixing their blood in the hybridization of a master race.

An important element in the Nazi mythos was the belief that representatives of a powerful, underground secret race emerged from time to time to walk among *Homo sapiens*.

Hitler's frenzied desire to breed a select race of Nordic types was inspired by his obsessive hope that it should be the Germanic peoples who would be chosen above all other humans to interbreed with the subterranean supermen in the mutation of a new race of heroes, demigods, and god-men.

Authors Louis Pauwels and Jacques Bergier quote Hermann Rauschning, governor of Danzig during the Third Reich, who repeated a conversation he had once had with Hitler concerning the Fuehrer's plan to assist nature in developing mutants.

"The new man is living amongst us now!" Hitler shouted. "He is here! Isn't that enough for you? I will tell you a secret. I have seen the new man. He is intrepid and cruel. I was afraid of him."

Rauschning stated that Hitler seemed to be in a kind of ecstasy as he spoke those words.

According to persistent rumors, there exists evidence to indicate that Hitler may have been mediumistic. Indeed, Hitler's birthplace, the little Austrian village of Branau-on-the-Inn, has long been a center of spiritualism in Europe; and it has been said that the infant Adolf shared the same wet nurse with Willy Schneider, who, along with his brother Rudi, became a world-famous medium.

Rauschning also claimed to have been told by a "person close to Hitler" that the Fuehrer often awoke in the night screaming and seized by convulsions. According to servants, the piteously whimpering dictator would cower and shout that "he" had come for him, that "he" stood there in the corner, newly arrived from his underworld kingdom to invade the Fuehrer's bedroom.

Adolf Hitler was not the only world leader who claimed to have received visitations from mysterious counselors. Although instead of being "new men," we might wonder if they were not representatives from a very old race.

The Red Man Appears to Napoleon in Egypt

According to occult tradition, an entity known as the "Red Man" first appeared to Napoleon during the ambitious military leader's Egyptian campaign. The strange visitor claimed to have warned the rulers of France in the past, and declared that he had now come to warn Napoleon.

When Napoleon protested the Red Man's admonition that the people of France were growing to fear his ambition, the mysterious advisor told the military genius that he had been at his side since he was but a schoolboy. "I know you better than you know yourself," he chided him.

The Red Man told Napoleon that his orders to the French fleet had not been obeyed. Even though the Egyptian campaign had begun on a note of triumph after the bloody battle of the Pyramids, the enterprise would fail and Napoleon would return to France to find her closed in by England, Russia, Turkey, and an allied Europe. Domestically, the Red Man warned, Napoleon would be confronted by the mobs of Paris.

True to the Red Man's prediction, the Egyptian campaign failed. In 1809, after the Battle of Wagram, Napoleon made his headquarters at Schonbrunn where, one lonely midnight, he again received his mysterious adviser.

The Red Man made his third and final appearance on the morning of January 1, 1814, shortly before the Emperor was forced to abdicate. The stranger appeared first to Counsellor of State Mole and demanded that he be allowed to see the Emperor on matters of urgent importance. Mole had been given strict orders that the Emperor was not to be disturbed, but when he went with the message that the Red Man was there, the mysterious stranger was granted immediate entrance.

It is said that Napoleon beseeched the Red Man for time to complete the execution of certain proposals, but that the prophetic messenger gave him only three months to achieve a general peace—if not, it would be all over for him. In a futile effort to gain more time, Napoleon desperately tried to launch a new eastern campaign. Such a move left Paris to fall into the hands of the Allies; and on April 1, three months after the Red Man's final appearance, Talleyrand and the Senate called for Napoleon's abdication.

Charles XII of Sweden Receives a Mysterious Visitor

Swedish folklore has it that King Charles XII of Sweden sought the counsel of a Little Gray Man with ruddy complexion, who gave him a ring that would not vanish until the day of the ruler's death.

King Charles cut a mighty swath across Europe, Russia, and Turkey, and his feats became legendary. Charles, too, resisted his mysterious counselor's entreaties to make peace.

In 1718, as the Swedes were besieging Fredrikshald, one of Charles's officers noticed that the ring was no longer on his leader's finger. Moments later, Charles fell dead with a head wound.

Washington's Valley Forge Angel

In the year 1777, a despairing George Washingon sat in his rude hut at Valley Forge. A movement in a corner of his room caused him to turn to see a rising, curling vapor surrounding a long-robed, long-haired entity, whom he first took for an Indian, but later decreed that it must have been an angel.

Washington told Anthony Sherman, a close friend, that the dark-complexioned angel had shown him a vision of

". . . the birth, progress, and destiny of the United States," although a printed account of the experience did not appear until 1888 in *The National Tribune*.

The Old Ones

There are persistent legends in nearly every culture that tell of the Old Ones, an ancient race who populated the earth millions of years ago. The Old Ones, an immensely intelligent and scientifically advanced race, are believed to have chosen to structure their own environment under the surface of the planet and to manufacture all their necessities. The Old Ones are hominid, extremely long-lived, and predate *Homo sapiens* by more than a million years.

The Old Ones are said to generally remain aloof from the surface people, but from time to time they have been known to offer constructive criticism; and it has been said that they often kidnap human children to tutor and rear as their own.

In virtually all the legends, the Old Ones have gone underground to escape natural catastrophes or the hidden death that exists in the life-giving rays of our sun.

A persistently propagated theory of Atlantis crosses the path of the Old Ones, the mysterious Teachers from the Caves; this theory declares that those Atlanteans who survived the great cataclysm learned to perpetuate themselves in underground caverns. This version of the destruction of the fabled continent has Atlantis shattering into the ocean as the result of a tremendous nuclear blast ignited by a self-destructive superscience. The necessity for finding underground accommodations was thus compounded by the deadly radiation on the surface of the earth, and by the knowledge that an existence away from the normal radioactivity of the sun is a healthier one.

The nemesis of radioactive fallout is, of course, a com-

paratively recent addition to the legend; but the explosion
of our own nuclear devices set off minuscule mushroom
clouds in the brains of thousands of Atlantis buffs, who
felt that they had at last been given the key to the reason
why the continent got lost in the first place: Atlantis had
been a nation of superscientists, who blew their continent
and themselves to bits.

Then, when UFOs began to be sighted in 1947, an
association between the underground survivors of a techni-
cally superior race and the flying saucers became obvious
to them: the Atlanteans were emerging from their subsur-
face kingdom to warn their suddenly dangerous successors
that nuclear power had the potential to destroy civilization.

Among the Amerindians, the Navajo legends teach that
the forerunners of the human race came from beneath the
earth. The ancient ones were possessed of supernatural
powers and were driven from their caverns by a great flood
(yet another echo of the traditional Atlantis myth). Once
on the surface, they passed along great knowledge to
humans before they once again sought secret sanctuary.

The Pueblo Indians' mythology locates their gods' place
of origin as an inner world connected to the surface people
by a hole in the earth. Mesewa, according to the Pueblos,
was succeeded as leader of the gods by his brother Oyoyewa;
this name, as some researchers have pointed out, is quite
similar to the Hebrew *Yahweh*.

For several years then, in one camp or another, Atlantis
has been associated with the Old Ones and the UFO
mythos: 1 An ancient hominid race antedating *Homo sapiens*
by a million years withdrew from the surface world, and
this physical withdrawal gave birth to the legend of Atlantis; 2 Atlantis, an actual prehistoric world of superscience,
blew itself to bits and its survivors sought refuge from
radioactivity under the crust of the earth; 3 Extraterrestrial
hominids, such as the Pleiadeans, planted a colony on
Earth, gave intellectually inferior *Homo sapiens* a boost up

the evolutionary ladder, then grew aghast at man's perpetual barbarism and withdrew to a more aloof position underground, thereby giving rise to the legend of Atlantis as a lost culture.

Extraterrestrials and the Egyptian Mystery Schools

Since most of the ancient legends described the visitors from the stars as having had a great influence on the Egyptian Mystery Schools, I asked Fred Bell if Semjase had provided him with similar information.

"Every 26,827.5 years," he explained, "Earth makes a rotation around the Pleiades and goes into a period of time wherein we come from a Dark Age, which is 12,000 years of the procession of the equinoxes, into the next 12,000 years, the dawning of the Age of Light. At that time, visitors from the Pleiades and other places have always come to lead us out of any mess that we might have gotten ourselves into.

"They will probably continue to do so until one of two things happens: (1) The planet goes into an environment such as Mars and the human race evolves from planet Earth to Jupiter, which is much like Earth was millions of years ago and would be the next place for us to live; or (2) We do some healing and extend the life of this planet, rather than destroying it every 25,000 years.

"The Pleiadeans influenced the mystery schools by the fact that there were direct visitations with some of the ancient people. It was a Pleiadean who is known in the Egyptian *Book of the Dead* as Osiris. He was said to have originally come to Mexico where he was known as the God of Agriculture, and where his other name was Quetzalcoatl. Then he moved over to Africa where he was misunderstood, and voodoo and black magic were created. Then he moved up into Egypt.

"The founding fathers of the Egyptian mystery schools were said to be offspring of the Pleiadeans, who lived on this physical planet and who had a lot to do with the guiding of Earth over the centuries. The Egyptians were a barbaric tribe in those times. At first they didn't understand the Pleiadeans who lived among them. But eventually the mystery schools, when they were founded, began to integrate Egyptian culture."

Did the Nazis Fly UFOs?

There are those researchers who contend very strongly that the Nazis *did* find their lost UFO and utilized its design for their own rocket technology. Interestingly, Fred Bell worked with Wernher von Braun at Rockwell.

"Wernher von Braun's father had a hunting lodge up in Peenemuende, that's where the Nazi space trip started," Bell said. "Von Braun was an interesting person to be around, but he never liked to talk very much. He didn't like Americans, because when he surrendered at the end of World War II, they put him in a concentration camp at White Sands, New Mexico, and left him there. They didn't bring him out until the Russians put their first heavy payload into orbit.

"As von Braun said, when the Americans and the Russians moved in on the caves in Peenemuende, the Americans took the Nazi plans and the Russians took the Nazi hardware. The hardware consisted of a hydrazine pump. The hydrazine pump made it possible for the powerful fuel distribution to get to the back of the engines and to lift those heavy payloads. The Americans had to start from scratch, because there were no plans for this particular pump."

Peenemuende, a small village on the isle of Usedom in the Baltic Sea, was the site of the Nazi rocket-aircraft experiment complex from 1937–45. Directed by Walter Dornberger and Wernher von Braun, German Army scientists at Peenemuende produced the V-2 rocket missile designated *Vergeltungswaffe* (revenge weapon), and the Air Force produced the V-1 missile. The scientific achievements of Peenemuende scientists, however, depended to a large degree upon previous German developments and postwar experiments with missiles, rockets, spacecraft, and aircraft.

It all began with *By Rocket to Interplanetary Space* (1923) by Hermann Oberth. Numerous other books had advanced the cause of spacecraft development in Germany during the mid-1920s. In 1927 the *Verein Fuer Raumschiffahrt* (VFR: Society for Space Travel) was created, with von Braun and Willy Ley among its members. The VFR produced the world's first rocket-powered automobile, the Opel-Rak 1, with Fritz von Opel in 1928. Further experiments were made with railway cars, rocket sleds, crude VTOL (vertical takeoff and landing) aircraft, and some successful rocket launches from the *Raketenflugplatz* (rocket airfield) near Berlin.

By 1933, when Adolf Hitler seized power in Germany, the government took over all rocket and aircraft development, and all astronautical societies were nationalized. Members had the choice of continuing their work under government auspices or becoming enemies of the Third Reich; thus the VFR dissolved officially.

In 1937 the Peenemuende group was formed, and until February 1945, when Peenemuende was evacuated, the Dornberger–von Braun team developed and conducted design work on a series of aircraft that were rocket-propelled and utilized certain gyroscopic principles for navigation and balance. A late stage of this series of vehicle, to be manned by a crew of two, was capable of *extremely* high altitude attainments, and was to be constructed in a *disk* shape. Unfortunately, this series of aircraft never reached construction stages, at least not while the Third Reich was in existence.

One of my UFO research associates, Jammie A. Romee, provided me with the following interesting "circumstantial evidence" regarding the Nazi UFOs. Shortly before the Third Reich collapsed in 1945, Wernher von Braun, Hermann Oberth, and about eighty other top scientists were smuggled out of Nazi Germany by the Allies. Documents, files, plans, photographs, designs, and so on were also spirited out along with the scientists. One specific file, containing the discoid-shaped aircraft designs, was also taken out of Germany—but not by the Allies.

The designs were destined to become part of a cargo that disappeared, as did one hundred thirty crack Nazi designers of specialized experimental aircraft.

This mysterious disappearance has been added to the following list of oddities which took place shortly before and shortly after the end of Adolf Hitler's Third Reich: (1) the unexplained disappearance of several German freight U-boats, capable of taking up to 850 metric tons each; (2) the disappearance from Tempelhof Air Base of several long-distance planes with flight plans to Spain and documentation to South America; (3) the disappearance of several tens of millions of marks in hard currency, gold bullion, and precious stones from the Reichsbank; (4) the fact that UFOs were, and are, sighted in great numbers over areas of South America in which many Nazis are known to be hidden; (5) the mass appearance of UFOs over Peenemuende; and (6) the fact that UFOs appear to avoid inhabited areas.

Super Science of the Ancients

I have long been fascinated by the legends of the Old
Ones, the Titans, or whatever one chooses to name them.
It is apparent that Egypt, the land of mystery for all those
interested in metaphysics and the occult, served as some
kind of ancient repository of wisdom for these alleged
ancient teachers of humankind. In the accounts of the
medieval alchemists we read of journeys to Egypt to seek
lost manuscripts and marvelous artifacts that would enable
those scholars to accomplish remarkable breakthroughs in
their fledgling sciences.

I have also researched the influence of the occult on the
formulation of the Third Reich, and I am convinced that it
was much more extensive than any of the "official" history books will probably ever admit.

If the great lost civilizations did exist, it may well be
that alchemy inspired by the Star Gods has served as the
connecting link between the extraterrestrials and our Atomic
Age. If one will manage to shake from his mind all
conceptions of the alchemist as a defrocked wizard or a
full-time fraud, he will discover that much more came out
of those smoky laboratories than candidates for the torture
chambers of the Inquisition.

In the intellectual half-light of the Middle Ages, we find
Albert le Grand, who produced potassium lye; Raymond
Lull, who prepared bicarbonate of potassium; Paracelsus,
who was the first to describe zinc and who introduced
chemical compounds in medicine; Blaise Vigenere, who
discovered benzoic acid.

Discoveries increased during the Renaissance when such
men as Basil Valentin discovered sulfuric acid, and Johann
Fredrich Boetticher became the first European to produce
porcelain.

Evidence has been disinterred from the musty alchemists' libraries in Europe which indicates that certain of the Medieval and Renaissance alchemists conducted experiments with photography, radio transmission, record phonographs, and aerial flight—as well as the endless quest to transmute lead into gold. The question is: How many of these experiments were successful?

In the seventeenth century, the Brethren of the Rosy Cross were rumored to have accomplished the transmutation of metals, the means of prolonging life, the knowledge to see and hear what was occurring in distant places, and the ability to detect secret and hidden objects.

Let us conjecture that there could have been a secret international society of "alchemists" which, centuries ago, gained a high level of scientific knowledge. Let us suppose that, hundreds of years ago, men of genius were given access to ancient manuscripts from advanced technologies and learned to duplicate many of the feats of the "giants."

Why would such people choose to keep such discoveries away from the rest of the world?

The answer may have been as simple as the appalling fact that most sincere alchemists, who took oaths to be pure in heart and inspired in their experiments by only the loftiest of intentions, were put to the torch by the Inquisition. Such dubious recognition would hardly be conducive to an uninhibited exchange of knowledge.

On the other hand, the alchemists' decision to form a society within a society may have been based on a highly developed moral sense that recognized the awesome position of responsibility in which the discovery of such applications of ancient, extraterrestrially inspired knowledge had placed them. Our hypothetical secret society might have decided to keep its own counsel until the rest of the world had caught up with its discoveries. These devout men may have bent their knees to pray that the rest of civilization might also, by that time, have developed a sense of moral awareness commensurate with its high degree of technical accomplishment.

The yellowed records of the alchemists remain in dusty libraries—more than 100,000 ancient volumes written in a code that has been deciphered sufficiently to convince scholars that such experiments *were* attempted. What if they succeeded?

What if certain men of exceptional intellect, power, and wealth actually achieved a high degree of technical accomplishments several centuries ago?

What if such men and women today continue to be guided in their research by alleged entities from other worlds or other dimensions?

I am intrigued by the allegation that the scientific apparatus discovered in the tomb of Christian Rosenkreuz (actual or symbolical founder of the Brethren of the Rosy Cross) is said to be common laboratory equipment for the 1980s but impossible apparatus for 1622. Had the alchemists actually attained a twentieth-century level of science in the seventeenth century?

Certain textbooks from the great civilizations of the past were preserved and hidden away by survivors of the cataclysm that destroyed their culture in about 5000 B.C. At that time certain of the primitive tribes in Egypt and Asia were evidencing signs of rudimentary civilization, and the survivors of the catastrophe journeyed to these lands and attempted to communicate the importance of these books to the more intelligent members of the tribes.

The Titans would have known that these people would not be able to comprehend the contents of the volumes for thousands of years, but the important thing was that the essence of a mighty civilization that had existed for nearly 10,000 years would not be allowed to vanish from the face of the Earth.

Doubtless hundreds of these precious volumes were either destroyed or neglected by the primitive peoples of the

Mediterranean and Asian cradles of civilization, but many of the priests to whom the Titans were said to have appeared interpreted the teachers to be divine and held the books in the highest reverence. It was because of these ancient priests, who had just a glimmer of the importance of the books attributed to the Titans, that we have been able to preserve this link with the world that existed before our own.

Some of the books were found nearly intact in mountain monasteries in Tibet. Fragments of manuscripts more precious than gold were discovered in China. It later became obvious that some early Egyptians of great genius had properly translated certain of the books supposedly written by the Titans centuries before; then, realizing the perishability of manuscripts, constructed more permanent clues to the book's secrets in the architecture of their pyramids.

As some schools have maintained, we have but rediscovered what the Titans had already known. It stuns the imagination to contemplate how much more we could accomplish if we had but one of their libraries intact!

An ancient Asiatic legend tells of the tradition of the Nine Unknown Men, who revealed nine areas of wisdom of the human race. It seems likely that the nine were Titans, who lived until their deaths in Asia and taught from their personal libraries to semireceptive Chinese and Indian cultures.

Fragments of these books were located in Buddhist temples and monasteries shortly after Marco Polo opened the door to the East for the European nations. The fragments were almost completely deciphered by an Italian alchemist in 1358, but his laboratory was destroyed and he was put to the stake by the Inquisition before he had effected a precise rendering of the code.

In 1529, an alchemist who was the son of a wealthy German prince and who became a cornerstone in the Protestant Reformation, made a final breakthrough when he completed the translation of several fragments and traveled to Tibet to bring back a copy of one of the original manuscripts attributed to the Titans. Monks had been laboriously copying the original for thousands of years with no idea of the importance of the manuscripts. Nor, of course, did they understand even a word of the language.

The book first held to be of greatest value was one which concerned itself with the transmutation of metals. Another deals with the rules for the evolution of societies, and the most effective means of government. There are volumes on microbiology, physiology, the control of gravitation, an analysis of light, various approaches to cosmogony.

The ninth book is devoted to the most incredible propaganda techniques and psychological warfare tactics conceivable.

The end result of the alchemist's science, as it was for the Titans', is the transmutation of the alchemist himself to a higher spiritual state. The ultimate goal of alchemy is the fusion of man with Divine Energy. The manipulation of matter is only a secondary concern.

10

Cosmic Soul Mates and Past Life Memories of Other Worlds

*S*ince Fred Bell often refers to Semjase as his "soul mate," I asked him what that term meant to him.

"The soul mate is the female aspect of your physical self," he answered. "In other words, it's like a twin—only in this case the twin wasn't born from the same mother. The twin comes from the same soul, the super soul, and merges with its counterpart.

"Sometimes the two will meet in physical incarnations and have time together. When they meet and leave their physical bodies at a certain point in the evolution of male and female nature, they become one spiritual being. The ego identity of the two merges into the ego identity of one. The Tibetans call this the *Mahabharata Mahat* principle. This is what it means to me."

Fred stated that he could not answer the question of whether we have more than one soul mate. "You might have many aspects of a female or male nature that would all synthesize in one. I'm sure they do, because let's say I find my soul mate and another person finds his soul mate. That combination of my soul mate, me as a *Mahabharata*, and the other person as a *Mahabharata*, reaches a higher plane of existence where we suddenly merge together because we're soul mates on that level. I think that's probably what's happening. It's kind of like the reverse of a fission, like a nuclear fusion principle.''

On the other hand, Fred noted, there are soul sisters and soul brothers, and these are people who have had ashramic experiences together. They've lived in ashrams together; they've worked in ashrams together—that is, they've performed work for God and for a group and they've become very close. Their vibrations have unified under the Master of the Ashram.

''A lot of times when you work in an ashram situation, you lose your identity and think that you're the master yourself—even though you're just an aspect of a server from the Master. This often happens when people take drugs. They realize that they've had an ashramic experience, and they think that they're Christ. Even though they're Christ beings, it doesn't mean that they are the Master.''

Our Soul's Mission on Earth

The Space Beings affirm the reality of reincarnation and inform their contacts that new incarnations may take place on any plane or planet during the soul's eternal life. According to the space intelligences' teachings, each newborn child has had aeons of life experiences and has come to Earth for a particular soul mission. One should not consider children to be newly created souls.

Contactees are advised that many of us living today have incarnated in families and other close groups because of ties formed in previous lifetimes, and we are to work together for a common spiritual purpose.

"When the time comes, in distant aeons, for the dissolution of this solar system, know that we have existed elsewhere long before coming here and that we will exist eternally somewhere," states a Mark-Age channeled message. "Consider also that the forces and the beings which comprise the structure of this solar system will be evolving to other levels and demonstrations in their own evolvements."

The Space Beings talk to the contactees a great deal about the "light bodies" of men and women on Earth. This term is not to be confused with either the soul or an illuminated physical body. As the Space Beings use the term, the light body is another name for the Christ or etheric body. In their theology, man's fall from grace refers to his loss of connection with his light body.

In the present age, as one comes into spiritual awareness and development, it becomes necessary to balance the mortal consciousness with the Christ consciousness until the light body becomes fully stabilized and begins to function with its full powers. When the light body begins to stabilize, the third dimensional body rises to a higher rate of vibration as the light body closes around the physical body and prepares to graduate to fourth dimensional frequency.

Past Lives on Other Planets

If there are "aliens" among us who remember certain aspects of their prior lifetimes, then that would explain the strange phenomenon that I began to notice in the altered-states regressions that I was conducting in the late 1960s and the early 1970s. It was at about that time that increasing numbers of men and women appeared to be reliving past lives on other planets or in other dimensions. Basically, I noted three general categories of claimed alien memories: the "Refugees," the "Utopians," and the "Energy Essences."

The *Refugee Alien* scenario surfaced from the regressed men and women who claimed memories of having come to Earth after they had fled their native planets because of great civil wars or cataclysmic natural disasters.

In some cases they seemed to recall having come to this planet on a kind of reconnaissance mission, and crash-landing here. In any case, they ended up trapped on Earth, unable to return to their home planet.

The *Utopians* seemed to form the largest category among my subjects. In the accounts given by regressed men and women, these aliens appeared to be deliberate planetary colonizers, who erected their space domes wherever they traveled in memory of the lifestyle on their worlds of origin. The Utopians were themselves dome-headed, suggestive of a highly evolved brain capacity, but were similar in all other recognizable aspects to *Homo sapiens*.

These "colonizers" could have served as direct ancestors of the subjects who spoke of them while in the trance state. I labeled them "Utopians" because the descriptions of their social and political structures seemed so idealistically perfect.

The *Energy Essences* were the strangest of all. Entranced men and women spoke of existences as disembodied entities of pure energy, yet with awareness. In a sense, they were mind-essences which were able to exist on even inhospitable, barren planets—or in space itself.

In my opinion, these entities were not at all to be confused with angelic intelligences. In many cases, these essences were said to drift rather purposelessly through space, or, in other instances, approached specific planets with the intention of inhabiting already existing physical bodies.

As I suggested, I gained the most information about the

Utopians. I heard of a planet with a reddish sky and with two moons. The cities and the individual homes were described as having been of crystal or some material which was crystalline in effect. The buildings appeared to have been translucent for the most part, but we also heard descriptions of the sun reflecting off spires and turrets. I was often told that the cities were sheltered under protective domes.

The subjects who recalled lives as Utopians under altered-states regression expressed a great nostalgia for the culture of that lost planet. The cities seemed to be run according to the ideals of a perfect democracy. Citizens enjoyed total freedom without the harsh by-products of civilization— crime, hunger, poverty.

A family unit in the manner that we know it did not seem to exist. Communal living, of a sort, seemed to prevail, although each person had his individual space and privacy.

Numerous subjects testified that the Utopians ate very sparingly, most often of a concentrated food that was made into a souplike mixture. The culture was completely vegetarian with no flesh foods of any kind being consumed.

My subjects most often remembered themselves as slender, quite short, with big-domed heads. Although they had little body hair and no beards or mustaches, they did mention longish golden hair and eyelashes. Their skin was most often said to be of golden brown complexion, and their eyes of a similar color.

While under trance, several subjects began to speak in a musical babble of language, which sounded very much like a cross between humming and talking in a singsong accent with a lot of "l's" and "m's" blended harmoniously. The Utopians had names like "Muma," "Lee-la," and "Lu-ah."

Music seemed to be an intrinsic element in their culture,

and I was told that it was primarily a free-form, nonrepetitive sound that often became a part of their thoughts.

In contrast to the tranquil, gentle lives of the Utopians, the Refugees' regressions were often filled with accounts of violent civil wars, burning cities, global holocausts. Many reported that they fled the planet before it exploded.

The accounts of a beleaguered, dying planet began to sound so reminiscent of tales of the legendary Atlantis that I speculated whether or not that memory, which seems so indelibly etched in humankind's collective unconscious, might not have actually occurred on another planet light years away in space.

Although the Refugees were generally less able to provide me with the kind of detailed information about their culture which the Utopians had given me, I found a number of these subjects concerned with the recall of anti-gravity devices, cancer cures, fireproofing formulas, and other advantages of their advanced technology.

Most of their memories, however, were cluttered with thoughts of survival and plans of escape from their doomed world. I did eventually manage to work with a number of subjects who seemed to have shared lives in the priestcraft of a temple on this planet, but they, too, remembered more of the destruction of the building than of their daily rituals.

Most typical of the Refugee regressions were graphic descriptions of immense portions of their planet being ripped apart by explosions, and large numbers of the population being annihilated. I also recorded several subjects describing fiery crash landings on Earth or on other planets, as their war-damaged spacecraft failed to negotiate proper landings.

At this point in my research, it would seem appropriate to add a fourth category to the alien memories. I have heard from increasingly large numbers of men and women who claim to recall coming to Earth for the express purpose of assuming incarnations on the planet as part of an extended mission of raising the level of humankind's consciousness.

Consider this claimed memory from a schoolteacher in Colorado:

"I am in a place of great light. Other 'beings' are there, although I cannot remember anything of their actual physical appearance.

"It seems that we are in a rather large, round object which hovers a short distance above Earth. I am shown a chutelike passageway leading downward, and I am given to understand that I am to go through this chute.

"My feelings about descending are not those of joy, but more like necessity or duty. This all seems to be part of the Plan. My last awareness is of passing downward . . . toward the Earth. There is no feeling of threat or danger, merely some sadness at separation from the other beings."

A woman secretary in a California school district remembers volunteering to come here on assignment from Galactic Command. Her role was to be that of one of a group of counselors who would assist Earth to evolve spiritually. On her planet of origin, she was a scientist who worked with channeling light as a source of energy.

According to her alien memories, her first life experience on Earth occurred in the Yucatán, where she was regarded as an oracle and where, for a time, she experimented with hypnotic drugs, which had been carefully devised to enable the native people to establish closer telepathic contact with her.

J. R. Ontario has his Ph.D. in Educational Psychology, and a belief in reincarnation to help explain in a balanced way the "strange things" which occurred to him as a youth:

"I understand that this is my first incarnation on Earth and that I volunteered to embark upon a specific mission, now nearing the completion of its first phase. I seem to remember myself in the past as an ethereal, rather than material, being.

"It is my understanding that it is my mission to discover and to develop the skills needed to help my fellow human beings, whether they are *Homo sapiens* or *Homo astrolis*, to 'overcome,' whatever this last word means."

A thirty-two-year-old contactee stated that he can recall each of his five previous lifetimes on this planet, and that in each prior existence he served as a contact point for UFO intelligences:

"On my native planet, I was a dream interpreter. I was sent to Earth to help prepare Earthlings for the coming UFO contact on a global basis.

"I lived in a city of light, of crystal buildings, where everything was peace and harmony. I used dreams to interpret any forthcoming health problems and to help people better understand themselves. We had conquered pain and suffering by our mental abilities—and these are gifts that we will one day be able to give to Earthlings."

A Cherokee physicist, who now lives in Alabama, not only had recall of a past life in the Pleiades, but was also able to fit his alien memories together with tribal legends that his people had come from another world:

"We lived in domed cities with translucent walls. We could fly, communicate with animals, transport ourselves instantly to other parts of our world.

"I remember our city as a golden color—a place of great beauty and calm.

"I came with others from my planet to help Earth through its birth pains into an intergalactic community and oneness. We were members of the priestcraft in ancient

Egypt; we were alchemists in the Middle Ages; we are scientists and clergy in the modern world.''

The whole matter of sensible men and women who claim alien memories invites extensive speculation.

Are these people, because of their higher intelligence and greater sensitivity, rejecting an association with Earth because of all the inadequacies and shortcomings which they witness all around them?

Does the mechanism of believing oneself to be of alien heritage enable one to deal more objectively with the multitude of problems which assail the conscientious and caring at every dawn of a new day?

But why do the alleged memories surface at such early ages? Why do these men and women recall an awareness of their ''true home'' long before they have begun to confront the harsh realities of successful existence on the planet?

Linda, a nurse from New York, recently left formal medicine so that she might become a spiritual healer.

''My earliest recollection is at the age of five,'' she said. ''For some reason I was very upset. I remember standing on the very top of my slide, looking up at the night sky. . . . I was just about hysterical as I looked up toward space. Through my tears I remember screaming: Come back, please! Don't leave me here with these barbarians. Why am I being punished so? This is not my home. These are not my people!

''I had an awareness that my people were leaving me behind. My world was the planet Orion.''

Linda is fortunate in that her husband is very understanding of her beliefs:

''He now knows and sincerely believes that I am an

alien. I've told him about my past lives on this world and my lives on other worlds.

"I have met a few . . . like myself, but only one remains in contact. The others are finding it very difficult to cope with their memories of our true Home.

"A woman named Monica remembers being a scientist from another world who participated in creating the first crude *[Homo sapiens]* of this world.

"Apparently, in this scientific work she did, she was cruel to these creatures.

"But something happened. She realized these creatures had feelings.

"I'll never forget how she looked when she told me how one of the creatures had taken her hand one day and caressed it. Monica realized then that just because one may have the knowledge to create a life form, it doesn't give one the right to *abuse* a life form."

Karen of Bricktown, New Jersey, identified herself to me as a "Starbaby." When she was seventeen, she set down thoughts which defined her differentness from her friends:

"I wasn't born here. My body must have been, but my soul and my mind are not of Earth. . . . It's almost as if two different beings are housed beneath my skull—the human part functioning just about all of the time; the alien part taking control but for a second or two, then disappearing once again into the background. But in that split second I see more, know more, than I have ever seen or known in a lifetime."

A Massachusetts social worker, a woman of Irish and French ancestry, remembers having lived on a planet called

Xanthro. She says the entities there were basically human-like in appearance, spoke a language known as Sumar, and sent emissaries to Earth to design the pyramids, which were "transmitters of an energy system known as Usan."

The social worker went on to inform me of her recollection of having been sent to Earth by a "Council of Twelve."

According to her thought: "We were responsible for the miracles recorded in the book of *Exodus*. We parted the Red Sea. Our craft created the columns of fire and of smoke which led the Israelites. We rained manna from the skies to feed the wandering tribes, and we even located water for them, cracking apart the ground to cause it to well up."

An industrial consultant from Arkansas vividly recalled his life as a "starcraft engineer" who was on board a vehicle that was forced to crash-land on Earth during an expedition to gather raw materials for industrial processing:

"All our systems were failing. We had lost most of our drive system, and we were preparing to die in the impact of the crash. . . . I could see the surface of Earth approaching.

"After crash-landing—in what is now northern Europe—we discovered that the pilots had managed to touch down with only minor damage. But tragically, although the engineering crew worked for months to attempt a repair, we could not get us spaceborne again. We couldn't even get our emergency signals to muster up enough strength to have a chance for rescue.

"I died in what is now Germany, and I lived several lifetimes on Earth prior to my present existence. I feel trapped here. I still want to get back to my home planet."

The Odyssey of the Spirit

Frederick Lenz, former professor of philosophy and author of the book *Lifetimes: True Accounts of Reincarnation*, told journalist Paul Bannister that out of about one thousand people whom he had regressed, several hundred had described life on other worlds.

Dr. Edith Fiore, a clinical psychologist and hypnotherapist from Saratoga, California, and author of *You Have Been Here Before: A Psychologist Looks at Past Lives*, told Bannister that she was convinced that some of her patients had lived before as aliens on other planets. What is more, she has been able to use certain data provided by such memories to cure her subjects of health or other problems.

Dr. Fiore recounted the case of a man, a nuclear engineer, who had great difficulty in memorizing things. Under hypnosis it was revealed that the man believed he had been a spacecraft pilot who had been assigned to transport a group of people from one planet to another. On one particular flight, he had been dismayed to learn, the craft designated for his use was an outdated model. Disgruntled, he flew it anyway against his better judgment.

"He directed the craft by mental projections," Dr. Fiore stated. "And at a critical time, a small child who was emotionally upset came to him from the passenger area. Because he was paying her attention, he forgot vital mental commands. He was forced to crash-land in a desert on Earth, and, during a trek to find water, both he and all his passengers died of thirst."

In spite of the tragic ending of what he recalled as that previous life experience, Dr. Fiore reported, she was able to use that knowledge "to help him remember things again—a direct application of past-life therapy."

If one accepts the eternality of the Soul and its evolutionary progression, why must such a return to the Source of All That Is be limited to physical expression lived only on the planet Earth?

If one accepts one God-Intelligence for the universe, why should each soul not experience that Divine handiwork wherever it manifests itself?

If one accepts a progression of lifetimes as opportunities for growth and for learning, why should we be confined only to the "classroom" of planet Earth?

Dr. Leo Sprinkle, director of counseling services at the University of Wyoming and an internationally acclaimed authority on past-life regressions of UFO encounters, told Paul Bannister that he had found "significant past-life experiences" on other planets.

"Although we cannot prove that it is true," Dr. Sprinkle admitted, "I am convinced that it is possible that some people have lived before as aliens. One other possibility is that these memories have been implanted in order to program us to prepare for life off this planet.

"These recollections are vivid and powerful, and I believe that these people are being sincere when they say these were their past lives. I have one woman who feels very angry. She feels she has been trapped here on Earth, and she just wants to get off the planet and return home."

Dr. Sprinkle is of the opinion that we should consider the enigma of alien memories from various standpoints.

"If we don't like the hypothesis that we have been seeded from extraterrestrial beings," he said, "we can still accept the hypothesis that somebody—our own subconscious, God, higher beings, *somebody*—is encouraging us to think in terms of space travel. We may be undergoing a process of mental programming by intelligent beings to provide us with guidelines so that in the future our children or our grandchildren will be able to go to other worlds."

Homesick for the Stars

For those whose personal cosmologies prohibit them from considering the hypothesis that some Earthlings might recall prior life experiences on other worlds, permit me to suggest another theory regarding why certain of us may feel so homesick whenever we gaze upward at the stars.

A number of scientists have been steadily amassing evidence that the Earth may have been seeded with life from outer space by means of meteorites, "shooting stars," that slammed onto this planet in some vast antiquity. These geochemists and astrogeologists have stated that within the fragments of certain meteorites they have detected predominant quantities of the kind of amino acids (the building blocks of proteins) that most commonly occur in living things. Although the concept is controversial, the implication of such research is that the beginnings of life on this planet were seeded by shooting stars.

If those essential sparks of life did indeed come from the cosmos, then we all would have good reason to feel nostalgia as we look up at the welcoming vastness of the night sky. And now, as we begin our first feeble attempts at leaving this planet to begin expanding our reach to other worlds, we should understandably know that we are returning home.

In the March 1982 issue of *Omni* magazine, Nobel Prize winner Dr. Francis Crick, the scientist who discovered the DNA molecule, spoke of his provocative theory that our planet had been "seeded" by intelligent life from a distant planet. Astonished by the uniformity of the genetic code on Earth, Dr. Crick conceived the theory of directed panspermia:

> Either you have a rocket manned with people who can
> somehow survive all that time through successive gen-

erations . . . or you need unmanned rockets carrying some other form of life. . . .

When you look at all of the options, it turns out that perhaps the most attractive one would be to send bacteria. They are small, and can be frozen for long periods of time, and can survive upon arrival under many adverse conditions that would kill more advanced life forms.

Sir Fred Hoyle, internationally recognized British astronomer and mathematician, has directly challenged the Darwinian concept of a gradual terrestrial evolution from some primordial ooze. In *Evolution from Space*, Hoyle, in collaboration with Chandra Wickramasinghe, states that life on Earth stemmed from microgenetic fragments from outer space which were "exactly the right size to ride on the light waves of stars."

The two British scientists declare that our planet received life with the "fundamental biochemical problems already solved." The source of such solutions was an intelligence whose purpose was to spread life "in an elegant way." This "intelligence" may be a series of question marks or may be God, Hoyle concludes, but "the new evidence points clearly and decisively to a cosmic origin of life on Earth."

There are other scientists who believe that consciousness of some sort exists in each living cell. There are evolutionists who theorize that at a certain stage of our development the individual cells and cell units that collected into our body parts all had consciousness, and that they deliberately formed groupings which evolved into a single unit with a unique life function and a collective sense of oneness. In other words, these millions of cells formed specialized organs, glands, muscles, bones, and so forth, which maintained a constant cooperative energy flow. The aggregate of their cooperation became a body, an "all." To a single cell, however, the all may be "God."

If the original cells of <u>life</u> on this planet came from outer space, then the memory of being "star stuff" which evolved to become humankind is an essential element in our species' collective heritage.

11

Becoming Attuned to Cosmic Vibrations

As part of their overall program to demonstrate to Earthlings that we are part of a cosmic whole—that we are free-flowing energy forms from the Father-Mother Creator of the universe—Space Beings are said to have decreed to the contactees that certain energies must be transmitted in order to accomplish a mass acceptance from the people and the leaders of Earth. Once this goal has been achieved, the extraterrestrials can accomplish the physical landings that they have been instructed to make on the Earth plane.

The contactees are confident that the Space Beings' energies will not overrule the desires of the human race nor interfere with the free will of contemporary civilization.

At the same time, though, the space intelligences have indicated that resistance to their instructions is steadily maintained by negative entities on the planet, which do not desire coordination in union with other worlds and other universes physically, spiritually, or mentally. Because of this resistance, our linkage with the space entities has been delayed. It was such resistance which may have prevented complete union in ages past.

Encountering Negative UFO Entities

Fred Bell has been instructed by Semjase that such negative entities do indeed exist, not only on Earth but in space. These otherworldly beings are little concerned about the welfare of humankind, and they commit such careless acts as entering Earth's atmosphere at "warp speed," thereby creating great stress upon our planet. In fact, Semjase stated, such a negative and thoughtless act not only disrupts Earth's atmosphere, but it releases "astral vampires."

These vampire-type creatures are seen usually after a UFO sighting. It is not that they're a product of a UFO being, but they are said to move through the time continuum just as UFOs do.

"Let's take the example of a heavy cruiser or a submarine traversing the Pacific Ocean," Fred explained. "Two weeks later, a reconnaissance helicopter or a dirigible flies over with infrared or heat-seeking equipment. Because of the sensitivity of the equipment they can actually measure where the ship was, even though it was there two weeks before.

"The same thing happens when one of these saucers moves over from one dimension to the other. When this occurs too close to our atmosphere or too close within our planetary environment, it will cause these creatures, which live on the astral realm, to move across.

"The higher beings, such as the Pleiadeans, won't cause their spacecraft to behave like that within the atmosphere of Earth. They might be invisible, but they won't move from one dimension to another because they know that

they'll create that kind of energy. They make their dimensional changes outside the astral field of a planet," Fred
continued.

"When these creatures are released due to the thought-
lessness of a Space Being, they claim that they are lost
entities. They are most dangerous for the first two weeks
after the full moon. That's when they seek out the sexual
organs of animals.

"They'll also seek out humans, but they somehow are
not able to penetrate the human field. Humans might act
crazy under attack by these vampires, but they don't get
their insides removed like the sheep or cattle do. The astral
vampires enter through the sexual parts of an animal, then
they materialize inside the cow or sheep or horse and drain
out all of the flesh and blood. When they go out again, the
animals just fall apart. I mean, there's nothing there but
skin and bones."

Many researchers have noted the correlation that seems
to exist between the appearance of UFOs and the cattle
mutilations that have been reported in the media. The
removal of the sexual organs is almost surgical in nature.
Mutilation is not the proper word.

"And look what happens down in the Bermuda Triangle
with this powerful energy," Fred continued. "Instead of
the extraterrestrials coming over here, we end up going on
the other side because there is a vortex that was created
back when Atlantis was destroyed. The capital city of
Atlantis was Poseidia, and it was right off the coast of
Florida where the Bermuda Triangle is. Poseidia left a
current of energy there."

In certain channeled material, the benevolent Space Beings
have indicated that they are coming into the atmosphere in
waves—just a little penetration at a time. They say this is
in order to prevent shock to the Earth's atmosphere.

The positive extraterrestrials emphatically state that they
will not land if the vibration would prove to be too much

of a shock to the already feeble and trembling Earth. But they indicate that they will continue to come close enough to be seen, and they explain that the darting lights, which we see and call UFOs, are now lowering into the atmosphere and preparing for a mass landing on the Earth plane.

The Transmutation of the Physical Body

Several UFO contactees have channeled the information that as the higher energy comes in, it will transmute the body cells, and will have effect not only on the physical, but also on the astral, mental, and emotional bodies. As the higher energy transmutes the physical body cells, they claim the old cells are destroyed or changed.

This is a normal process, of course; but according to Mark-Age, with the higher and increased energy influx, the process is stepped up considerably.

The destruction of old cells often causes various degrees of discomfort, pain, and strange sensations in the functioning body. Mark-Age channeling says that it also causes strange mental and emotional disturbances, involving soul memory patterns, beliefs, and desires. All of this must be taken into consideration when analyzing, coping with, treating or resolving, and aiding the necessary spiritual changes now being brought upon all of humankind upon Earth.

"For truly time and the processes of ending an old age, so as to begin a new age, are being shortened for the elect," Mark-Age declares. "All of us are being affected by it; but we are in physical bodies of a three-dimensional nature upon Earth. If we can understand what is happening and what we can do about it, we sometimes can aid, rather than hinder, the process. And sometimes we even can accept the pains, the uncertainties, the torments, and the doubts better."

Mark-Age suggests that the process of increased physical change uses much of the body's protein, calcium, and B vitamins, and their channels urge that the nutrients be replaced as soon and as completely as possible. The acceleration also causes abnormally high elimination of waste products. Nerve information is also affected.

Mark-Age has assembled a list of some of the effects which they have noted as people came to their Foundation in Miami, Florida.

They have recorded mental effects, in which people begin to lose their enthusiasm and become very apathetic. They've noticed emotional effects, in which the individual gives voice to strange fears and to complaints of stresses and strains without apparent cause; and becomes irritable, argumentative, and desires to cry at the slightest provocation.

Mark-Age has also observed physical effects—people complaining of difficulty in getting to sleep soundly or difficulty in waking fully; of pains in various parts of the body, such as the head, the lower back, the leg nerves; of stiffness in the hands and feet; of discomfort in the chakra areas, including the heart, throat, solar plexus, and sacral plexus.

In addition to meeting their increased need for more protein, calcium, and B vitamins, Mark-Age urges that individuals today get plenty of liquids in order to flush out their bodies.

Many contactees have noticed an apparent acceleration of time. Time is just going too fast for too many people.

These contactees believe there are also physical, mental, and emotional purgings due to the continuing influx of energies. There are mass cleansings, as Earthlings resist correction and self-examination. It becomes harder and harder to face the importance of the "Latter Day period."

There is also said to be a general aura of impatience in which important things seem not to be developing as fast as one would like.

The Realignment of Humankind

Aleuti Francesca, of the Solar Light Retreat in Central Point, Oregon, sees the suffusion of new energies on the planet as seeking to realign humankind and to reposition the physical aspect of people so that they have a greater opportunity to link up with the Space Beings.

"All light workers who are developing extrasensory perceptions and telepathic abilities, what you term clairvoyance, clairaudience, clairsentience (and even communication in the dream state), must be heightened insofar as the necessity will be present for the linkup through the inner, rather than dependence on the outer, senses," space intelligences told Ms. Francesca. "All these things must take place swiftly now upon the planetary scene as events are moving at a much greater speed than man anticipates—or will recognize in his conscious mind—until these events force themselves upon his attention on a very physical and obvious level."

A representative of space intelligence channelled through Aleuti Francesca:

"We have previously commented to you upon the two extremes of manifestations of the inflowing light energies—that of a greater breaking up of old constructs or the destructive processes already set in motion, and a greater upliftment and an expansion of consciousness with all who are aligning themselves at a spiritual level with the incoming energies. Do not be surprised, therefore, that a division will take place among the peoples of your planet between those who go onward in light and those who become even more enmeshed in the level of materialistic existence.

"Nothing remains static. Everything moves at a very fast and accelerated pace; therefore, that which does not move forward, falls back. That which does not expand and become uncrystallized, unlimited in consciousness, falls back into a greater crystallization and will, therefore, be shattered as the energies rebound throughout all molecular structures.''

There Is but One Ultimate Creator

Ray Mere, an entity who sometimes communicates through Aleuti Francesca, has said that humankind must be prepared so that it can see the necessity of reaching out through the spiritual force to a Creator. Humankind must recognize in the existence of cosmic law and of planetary law the existence of one ultimate Creator of all beings.

Ray Mere tells us through the channel that we should not delude ourselves by thinking that the vast masses of the peoples on this planet have yet reached this stage. If this were so, Ray Mere observes, conflicts on the surface of Earth would have ceased between nations and peoples and ideologies; and there would no longer exist starvation, suffering, and agony, which still hold many millions of peoples of the Earth in thrall. Only when there is a realization of the spiritual nature of humankind can there come about an end to its suffering. Humankind must move forward in one united goal toward the reclaiming of a planet sadly damaged by violence, selfishness, and mismanagement.

''The mission of all peoples who term themselves servers of the light, interplanetary emissaries, servants of God, is that of enlightening those who yet walk in darkness through all means available to them,'' Ray Mere said. ''When the time is appropriate in the skies of Earth, there will be the showing of vast numbers of our craft so that Earthman may look upward and see that beings and races from other planets approach, and that the law of the Confederation comes to the assistance of the brothers and sisters of Earth.''

Ray Mere says that the Space Beings are with Earthlings in consciousness and that their energies are reaching forth to us.

"Open up in consciousness to the fullest extent possible, and you will find vast inrushes of energy of a highly creative nature. Guard against opening yourselves to negative energies of any type whatsoever, as these will result in the tearing away of stability.

"You are brothers and sisters, and you have a far greater responsibility than you may yet be aware. Until a certain point of time is reached, we cannot intervene openly in the affairs of your planet. Until that time, you are as our hands and feet. Through you flow the energies which will determine the direction in which events will move.

"You recognize, of course, that when we speak to you as Children of Light, we do not speak only to you, the small group gathered here, we speak to the greater audience to whom our words shall reach as these go forth. For this transmission is needed and directed toward the greater listening public, who are the Children of Light throughout the planet.

"Our light is ever with you. The light of the one Creator shines forth and may be reached more simply than ever before, as the crystallized molds break and shatter upon the planet and as old realities come into consciousness to be transmitted in light.''

Increa/ed Vibratory Pattern/

Xyclon, a "space psychologist," channeled his comments through the Solar Light Center; his subject was the impact of the increased vibratory patterns of energy upon the consciousness of individuals making up the face of planet Earth.

It is reported that Xyclon said that the Space Beings were closely watching the reactions of masses of people to the tremendously stepped-up outflow of energy which is now reaching Earth from other levels of existence. Xyclon commented that when there was in the consciousness of individuals an awakened state of soul, there was an actual linkage which took place between the higher intelligences and the brains of Earthlings. When this awakened consciousness is not in existence, Xyclon explained, there is an actual breaking down of the cellular structure.

"Where the awakened consciousness does not yet exist in the soul of the individual, a breaking down of the cellular structure is taking place by virtue of the tremendously high frequency rate of energies flowing in from the central sun source," Xyclon stated. "I would say that a state similar to one of friction is taking place. It is known to you that the cells contain a level of consciousness or awareness of their own in that each cell is as an individual planet within a galaxy, making up the aggregate of consciousness to the individual.

"Where there is not an awakened level of soul, the consciousness level of each cell is at a slower or more dense rate of vibration," Xyclon continued to channel through Ms. Francesca. "Due to this, as the increased high-frequency energies pour in, a state close to that of friction is reached, and a kind of heating process is produced which results in a high level of irritability or discomfort or disease within such an individual.

"Conversely, as we have previously told you, we are individuals of a highly awakened consciousness level, gathered together to raise even higher the vibratory level of consciousness. In harmony and understanding, there comes about a condition wherein the light energies flowing in do so to such an extent that the miraculous may take place.

"At such times, not only will you find what are termed miraculous healings of the physical, etheric, emotional, and mental bodies taking place, but you will find that in this raising of the vibratory rate to these high levels, periods of spiritual exaltation in a knowingness of the infinite nature of man and his destiny of light becomes manifest to the individuals concerned.''

The Negative Counterforce of Radiation

In addition to expressing excitement and enthusiasm for the new regenerating energies being beamed toward Earth by the Space Beings, certain channels are relaying warnings from the entities regarding various negative energies being released by humans and their sciences.

In a channeling received by Lucille McNames of Huntington Beach, California, the extraterrestrials reportedly warned not only of ultrahigh-voltage power line leakage, but the deadly radiation blasted by our nuclear testing programs—radiation which is currently finding its way into bodies of our water, into our foodcrops and our atmosphere.

"We are at a loss to comprehend why Earth medical men cannot see how the deadly effects of such radiation seepage can harm humankind. Radiation is not only giving more power to the dark forces, but causing strange, virulent diseases in man, deeply affecting his brain cells, anatomic and molecular system, and blood circulation, imbalancing the red and white cells,'' the extraterrestrials have been quoted as saying to Ms. McNames.

"For years, we have urged scientists to stop this atomic blasting that upsets nature's own cyclic rhythm, or suffer the consequences.

"We urge scientists immediately to begin to regulate their ultrahigh powerlines all over the globe, and to stop atomic testing if man wants a chance for survival. We urge doctors and UFO research people to break through intellect to truth, as we know truth.

"We urge all those who read these messages to protect yourselves twenty-four hours a day by visualizing a white Christ shield around your bioplasmic surround. See this light protecting your family, friends, and fellow man. Radiation is the work of diabolical forces. Fight back with light. This is the time to be stronger than you thought possible. Join us, the light forces. We are your lifeline."

A Pathway of Enlightenment

The following material was channeled by Robert Short of the Blue Rose Ministry, Cornville, Arizona. Short, who has been a medium for UFO intelligences for many years, identifies the communicating entity as Korton:

"There now grows in the consciousness of the people of your planet an awareness of a *degree of initiation* into the discipleship of light and peace. Those who are now on this *pathway of enlightenment* will soon find their thoughts withdrawn from the everyday consciousness. We are most aware of those who choose the *pathway of enlightenment* as set forth by the teachers of our school of philosophy, which is indeed ancient by your standards. Be advised to walk among men on your planet as observers of the deeds of man, but not necessarily partakers of those deeds, which do no honor or justice to the dignity and birthright of man. Indeed, the Spiritual nature of man is much removed from the ordinary common ways of most of those who must deal in matters of state.

"In order to achieve perfect *peace* and a *noble way*, and to receive teachings invaluable to the initiate on the *pathway*, the initiate submerges his/her physical personal self in deep meditation and thus he/she achieves, as it were, a *state of union* with his or her innermost nature and thus is free to receive the teachings at the feet of the Master, then to relate this to other pupils and novices of the pathway in the worldly sense. For without this meditation and peace, your world would be bereft of prophets, teachers, and lesser instructors of teaching. For one to honor and to covet the various faculties inherent in one's inner nature, it is necessary that they retire into a state of meditative reflection. Knowledge of the innermost being gives knowledge of the worldly teacher. The student becomes the disciple; the disciple becomes the world teacher.

"No Master or teacher has become so by mere application of good deeds or words spoken. The true teacher is one who has literally uplifted into enlightenment those over whom he has charge, thereby saving those who would be sacrificed to the lower element of the gross physical nature of flesh.

"The Master must at all times 'come to grips,' so to speak, with the temptations of man, and yet be above such temptations to the point of understanding their nature. The Master must achieve this balance without fear of temptation, yet remain compassionate toward those who have as yet little understanding of their participation on the great stage of life patterns and soul growth.

"One must not be above those who cry out for enlightenment. One must not be deafened to the call which goes out upon the ethers of your planet and speaks with a *hidden word* into the ear of the chosen student-novice, who then breaks from form and begins to look upon *all* as being a *state of formlessness becoming perfection*. From such a source flows an enlightenment of consciousness.

"You who read these words are in that consciousness that requires your attention and your meditative reflection in order to hear the words of your Master in a voice commanding, yet gentle. When you hear your call upon the ethers, answer, 'I am here, Master, and wish to serve those who serve our Radiant One, Ageless Light and Life.'

"The key to all of the law is to work with humility, and yet be knowledgeable in all things so that man might respect the majesty and the dignity of wisdom and know that he or she is in the presence of one who sits at the feet of the Master forever. The *'Word'* and the enlightenment of knowledge is passed through the process of student becoming initiate, thereby consummating such knowledge by graduating to Masterhood.

"Remember to choose a time for your meditation when you are well rested, alert. Your ears should be unstopped, and your eyes fully open to those *truths* which will come pouring forth into your mind. Be among those who shall say, 'I am the learner who is ready to receive the word of the Master, which will live within the heart of my being. My centers are fully awake, vibrant with the rhythmic breath of life which flows outwardly and inwardly. I am on the pathway of one who serves, and I am numbered among the many disciples on the PATHWAY OF ENLIGHTENMENT.'

"We wish you to know that there are *many lives* that are to be lived not only on your planet, but also upon other worlds. You have lived many lifetimes of what is called 'good,' and other lifetimes which are the opposite of good. This has been for your own experience, one of *balance* and the other *imbalance*.

"Do not seek after material goods or power, but seek to gain in spiritual growth and potential. We would advise that one live according to natural and spiritual laws, even as our people on other worlds live. *Be fair to all whom you meet. Live with justice, ethics, and morals*, which you mete out to yourself, as well as to those with whom you come into contact. *Fear not*, and walk in the way of those who always seek the TRUTH of all things. Thus you shall always be in the minds and hearts of the learned Masters."

12

Testament for a Space-Age Religion

In the view of many UFO researchers, scriptural sources provide an untapped area of space data which was produced through the process of revelation. Even though the Bible was not written as a source book on outer space, it contains many important conclusions on cosmic matters which presently lie beyond the reach of contemporary science.

"I believe in space religion," a Seventh Day Adventist clergyman told me, "because the Bible indicates that we are going to spend eternity in space. In a sense, Jesus is a spaceman.

"The writers of Biblical times were at a disadvantage in describing sophisticated spacecraft," he went on. "For lack of other terms they resorted to their only known word for a vehicle of transportation—'chariot.' "

Those who have conducted a careful analysis of Biblical texts have found three types of cosmic conveyances employed as vehicles of transportation for intelligent beings:

the wheel, or disk-shaped object described by Ezekiel; the chariot of fire mentioned in the second book of Kings; and the cloudy chariot found in the writings of Moses, Daniel, David, Matthew, Paul, and John.

In II Kings 2:11–12, 6:17; Psalms 68:17; and Habakkuk 3:8, the Bible describes a cosmic craft identified as a "chariot of fire" powered by engines called "horses of fire" with "charioteers" (pilots). The chariot's lift-off is called a "whirlwind."

In II Kings we read: "And it came to pass, when the Lord would take up Elijah into heaven by a whirlwind, that Elijah went with Elisha from Gilgal . . . and . . . behold, there appeared a chariot of fire, and horses of fire, and parted them both asunder; and Elijah went up by a whirlwind into heaven. . . ."

In Zechariah 6:1–7, four cosmic pilots are dispatched in as many spacecraft (chariots) which come out "from between two mountains." The prophet is informed that each charioteer had flight orders to go to a different part of the country. According to scripture, the four had been ordered to "walk to and fro through the earth." The Confraternity Version of the Bible (Roman Catholic) reports that the orders were: "Go patrol the earth."

Isaiah 19:1 records that ". . . the Lord rideth upon a swift cloud."

Moses frequently mentioned the cloud-chariots: "The Lord descended in the cloud"; "The Lord came down in a cloud"; "The Lord went before them by day in a pillar of cloud to lead them the way; and by night in a pillar of fire."

The prophet Daniel was another who described the use of a cloudy chariot for cosmic transportation. And, in the New Testament, Matthew recorded the sighting of a cloudy chariot during the Transfiguration—"a cloud composed of light enveloped them (Moses, Elijah, and Jesus) with brightness."

At his Ascension, Jesus was transported in a cloudy chariot. "And when he had spoken these things, while they beheld, he was taken up; and a cloud received him out of their sight" (Acts 1:19).

Certain UFOlogists have pointed out that this was no ordinary cloud because it is identified by the author, Peter, as a chariot.

In his Revelation, John further demonstrated that the cloudy chariot was more than an ordinary cloud and could support the weight of an object heavier than air when he wrote that Jesus "sat on the cloud" (Revelation 14:14–15).

Angels from Outer Space

In both the Old and the New Testaments, we are told that there are unseen intelligences that are divided into two vast hosts: the one, obedient to God and active in good ministries for man, called angels; the other, intent on annoying and harming man and loyal to Satan, called demons.

UFO contactees often refer to the same dualism. There are Space Intelligences who seem negative, even hostile, toward the goals of evolving humankind. There appear to be, as the ancient texts proclaim, "Sons of Light" and "Sons of Darkness."

Such a division also reminds us of Edgar Cayce's concept of the primal warfare on Atlantis between the beneficent Children of the Law of One and the evil Sons of Belial. Belial, by the way, is Hebrew for "person of baseness," and the name is used to designate the prince of devils, Satan.

The term *angel,* as used in scripture, is used to designate an office, rather than to describe a person. An angel, simply, is a messenger, one who is sent to accomplish whatever mission is assigned to him. Any student of the

Bible can readily testify that angels are referred to as actual beings and not simply impersonal influences.

Angels ate with Abraham, were lusted after by the Sodomists, grasped Lot by the hand. They refuse to be worshipped by humans, but they never turn down hospitality. The manna of Israel was "angel's food," the "bread of the mighty."

Angels stand in relation to God, the Supreme Being, as courtiers to a king. They are not gods, but are themselves created beings, as subject to God's will as are people.

And angelic ranks were formed long before humankind was scooped from the dust of Earth.

Although they are frequently called spirits, it is often implied in the Bible that they have corporeal bodies, but dwell on a higher plane of existence than humans. Luke 20:36 states that the redeemed in the resurrection will be "equal unto the angels." In other words, men and women shall be raised to those conditions common to those beings who now enjoy certain metaphysical advantages.

When seen on Earth, angels have always appeared youthful, physically attractive, commanding; and they are described in much the same manner as UFO contactees of today describe their "Space Brothers and Sisters." Even though angels may be mistaken for ordinary humans when judged by their appearance alone, those who have confronted them have often felt the physical effects of their majesty.

Their appearance is often sudden and accompanied by a bright light. Saul of Tarsus and the guards about Jesus' tomb were blinded by the light of the angels. One touch of an angel's hand crippled Jacob. The single stroke of an angel's staff consumed Gideon's offering. Zacharias was deafened by an angel's word. Daniel's men fell to quaking at an angel's voice, and the shepherds were overawed by the angelic aerial display that heralded the birth of Jesus.

Whenever angels are mentioned, they are described as

strong, swift, splendid, subtle as the wind, elastic as the light. No distance wearies them and no barriers hinder them. To Abraham they appeared suddenly, without announcement. An angel entered the fiery furnace to keep Shadrach, Meshach, and Abednego cool, and another entered the lions' den with Daniel and closed fast the jaws of the beasts.

The invisible world of the angels seems to be one filled with daily tasks and graded authority. When Gabriel appears to Zacharias to announce the coming birth of John the Baptist, he identifies himself as one who stands in attendance to God. He seems to be saying that just as Zacharias was a priest in a temple on the earth plane, so likewise was he a priest in a temple in a higher realm.

The angel who appeared to Gideon seemed to be a military specialist and promised to guide the Israelite in his rebellion against the Midianites. Zechariah, the prophet, had so many lengthy discussions with an angel that he surely must have encountered a heavenly philosopher.

Then there are the fierce angels who specialize in meting out punishment—those who brought the ten plagues to Egypt; those who threw down fire and brimstone on Sodom and Gomorrah. When Sennacherib strutted in defiance with his mighty armies, an angel descended and, in one night, slew 180,000 Assyrians. We are told in II Kings that the angel's means of destruction was to "send a blast upon him," a hot smothering wind.

Since the Creation, the angels have manifested an active interest in the affairs of *Homo sapiens*. Job 38:7 tells us how the "sons of God" shouted aloud when the Lord laid the earth's foundations, settled its dimensions, and set its supporting pillars in place. Moses received the Sinaitic law from the mouths of angels (Galatians 3:19), and the Psalms tell us how angels have control of nature's laws (103:20, 104:4).

Throughout the scriptures one caution is given man concerning the angels: He is not to worship them.

In Revelation, John, its author, seeks to worship the angel who has shown him a vision of heaven. He is stayed in this action by the angel, who says, "See thou do it not: I am thy fellowservant, and of thy brethren. . . ." (19:10). Essentially the same admonition is repeated in 22:9, when John once again seeks to kneel at the angel's feet: "I am thy fellowservant . . . thy brethren . . ." Although they are quite willing and quite capable of aiding man in his crises, they consistently emphasize that they are brothers to man, not gods. The space intelligences have continually underscored a similar admonition to the UFO contactees of today.

Quite a different relationship exists between humanity and the fallen angels, the servants of Satan (Belial). The doctrine of demons is abundantly and decisively taught in scripture, from the serpentine devil deceiving Adam and Eve in the Garden of Eden to the demonic harassment of Jesus and the demons' promise of continued warfare against all those who seek to do good.

The Bible makes it quite clear that Satan and his minions had some connection with Earth before man appeared on its soil, and that Satan and his hosts had already fallen from grace. If Satan were once God's vice-regent on Earth, perhaps his declaration of war against *Homo sapiens* stems from his jealousy of his successors. For in Genesis 1:26–28 God declares: "Let man have dominion over all the earth, and over every living thing that moveth upon the earth."

According to the account of the Garden of Eden, it surely did not take Satan long to begin showing man up as a naive, bungling simpleton, a most ineffectual successor indeed.

It appears evident that we have two distinctly different kinds of angels about us in the invisible world which surrounds our own. Of one type of angel it is written that "they neither marry nor are given in marriage," which implies one of two things: Either they are basically ethereal creatures whose company neither dies nor multiplies; or they are corporeal creatures who avoid direct contact with, and physical exploitation of, a primitive species. They would appear to follow a strict intergalactic law not to interfere with the physical evolution of a planet.

We learn more of the earthly apostate angels in the apocryphal Book of Enoch, which even fundamentalist biblical scholars recognize as valuable for bequeathing us a tradition of great antiquity. In Enoch we read: "It happened after the sons of men had multiplied in those days, that daughters were born to them elegant, beautiful. And when the angels, the sons of heaven beheld them, they became enamored of them, saying to each other: Come, let us select for ourselves wives from the progeny of men and let us beget children" (7:1,2).

Later, "The valley of the angels who had been guilty of seduction, burned underneath its soil. . . ." (66:6,15).

"Those who seduced them shall be bound with chains forever" (66:39).

It appears that there may be an angelic police force which punishes those of its kind who abuse certain cosmic laws regarding attitudes and actions against *Homo sapiens*. According to Enoch, there were certain "angels" who wished to exploit humankind for their own ends. And so it seems to be today, when UFO contactees are warned of negative astral entities who wish to keep our species isolated from our benevolent Space Brothers.

A New Age of Mainstream Mysticism

A Gallup Poll conducted late in 1976 indicated trends which appeared to point to a spiritual revival in the United States. Sales of religious books were higher than ever before, and church or synagogue attendance reflected an upturn for the first time in two decades.

But an even more significant departure from earlier religious polls lay in the increasing number of Americans who had developed an interest in the inner or spiritual life. Three out of ten surveyed believed that they had had at least one experience of leaving the body and returning, of a Oneness linkage with a Higher Consciousness, of mental communication with the living, of contact with the dead. A projected six million men and women were participating in, or were involved with, transcendental meditation; five million practiced some form of yoga; three million were participants in the charismatic movement; three million practiced some form of mysticism, and two million had become adherents of Eastern religions.

In 1982 a Gallup Poll revealed that one out of every four Americans believes in reincarnation and that 43 percent reported having an unusual or inexplicable spiritual or religious experience. In 1985 the Roper Poll showed that 74 percent of Americans believe in the afterlife; 50 percent accept the reality of ESP; and 41 percent think that there is life somewhere else in the universe.

Dr. Martin E. Marty, historian of religion at the University of Chicago and a veteran observer of the contemporary American religious scene, commented to the Chicago *Tribune* [1976]: "I would use a picture of religion as if it was tied up in a balloon." Continuing the analogy, he said, "The amount in the balloon never changes. But if you press your hand on it, it simply bobs up between the fingers and takes a different shape, depending on the time or place.

"In the 1950s, religion took a surprising institutional twist. Everybody was moving to the suburbs, and they were building big churches. It was the thing to do.

"In the 1960s, everyone was as religious as always, but it took the shape of 'elites' being interested in Teilhard de

Chardin, the Second Vatican Council, radical theology, or the Martin Luther King movement. And institutions suffered.

"Today I see things very much in the language of the inward journey, the private search, the individual quest, and *ad hoc* four-, five-, or six-person get-togethers."

A survey directed by Catholic priest and sociologist Andrew Greeley, of the National Opinion Research Center at the University of Chicago, stated that in a sampling of 1,500 Americans four out of ten reported having a so-called "mystical experience," which was defined as feeling as though one were very close to a powerful, spiritual force that seemed to lift one out of oneself.

The Chicago *Tribune*'s own survey found that about two out of ten Chicagoans admitted ". . . they had been lifted out of themselves at least once." The experience had been triggered, many said, by such diverse happenings as "solitary contemplation, physical exercise, childbirth, watching the sun set, lovemaking, reading the Bible, or listening to music."

American Health, January/February 1987, carried Father Andrew Greeley's scientific survey of Americans and their interactions with the paranormal. Dr. Greeley and his colleagues at the University of Chicago have been assessing the growing rate of mysticism in the populace since 1973. The priest-sociologist is currently a professor of sociology at the University of Arizona in Tucson. Among the findings detailed in his report, "Mysticism Goes Mainstream," are the following:

Nearly half (42 percent) believe that they have had contact with the dead. Widows who claim an interaction with their deceased husbands number a remarkable 67 percent. Not surprising, however, is that 73 percent of all the men and women polled believe in life after death.

Twenty-nine percent of those interviewed admitted to having visions. The number of those indicating ESP experiences climbed to 67 percent of the total.

Dr. Greeley suggests that such great numbers of people expressing freely their mystical experiences could change the nature of our society. Specifically germane to the subject of this book is his comment that as many as twenty million Americans have undergone "profoundly religious moments of ecstasy" and report "out-of-body trips, being bathed in light, or other encounters that transformed their lives." Such men and women, Dr. Greeley states, "become profoundly trusting, convinced that something good rules in the world."

UFOs, Science, and Religion

The messages of the contactees seem to be part of the national religious trend to go within, to enter the private search, and to embark upon the individual quest; they seem, also, part of a determined effort to bring God, his agents, or other worldly emissaries back into the role of active participant in the affairs of humankind.

Contactee Aleuti Francesca commented, "I not only feel that the contact with extraterrestrials is an important factor in the merger of science and religion, I feel that is the single *most* important factor to emerge on the world scene in the last two thousand years.

"Man is on the brink of tremendous changes and breakthroughs, and *only* New Age Man, transformed man, can make it through to a new world and a spiritually sane existence. Transformation from matter into Light, from the physically dense body structure to the Light Body structure, is the leap ahead for mutated man."

Wayne S. Aho is president and founder of the New Age Foundation of Eatonville, Washington, and has been an emissary of UFO and New Age teachings for nearly forty years. He said, "I believe that there are beings who keep up with the progress in all parts of the universe, and assistance is given to move planets and peoples ahead. The Earth is especially in need of this assistance in order to overcome wars and strife.

"I believe that eternal truths live, that earlier seers and prophets taught this age-old wisdom, and that it is revealed to us again by new 'receivers'—for even prophets 'come again'—for the purpose of edifying our Earth right now. Religions tend to crystallize; thus new approaches are given; new ways of saying things that have always been true are developed; and mankind progresses.

"No place in the Universe can afford to be stagnant," he added. "Progress is a way of life everywhere. Thus, in this present day, visitation has revived learning and spiritual growth."

Does Wayne Aho foresee the blending of science and religion?

"I believe that there is *one truth;* and in order to bring harmony on Earth, religion and science will have to combine," was his response.

What is Aho's own personal assessment of the nature and scope of his mission?

"I believe that I am to function as a New Age teacher, bringing cosmic realization of the universe to those ready to receive it. This includes healing, as well as sharing truths in science and religion," he said.

"I am very interested in new energy systems based on the truths evident in the Cosmos and proved by UFO visitation. We live in a time of challenging change and world crisis. Through my work, I am hopeful that more unification and harmony will come between all peoples for the good of the planet. I have made a personal dedication which has been fulfilled in a million miles of travel for a period of over twenty years of lectures, conventions, and other programs."

Does Aho see the UFO as an important factor in the

merging of science and religion? Does he accept the UFO as a transformative symbol of universal spiritual experience?

"The Earth is rising again from the Dark Ages and enlightenment is coming very rapidly," Wayne Aho said. "Open minds are receiving and discovering new insights into the purpose and meaning of life. Earth will continue; life will continue, albeit great changes are immediately ahead.

"UFOs have a unique place in this change, inasmuch as no one can claim to know the total answer about them. No one can really argue against the postulation of new ideas, for the new ideas just might be right. In this way, the UFO is leading human progress out of crystallized thought forms or presently accepted religious life concepts. Man will grow, and new truths will emerge."

One Religion

Bertie Catchings, a psychic-sensitive and contactee from Dallas, Texas, said that the goal of the New Age is for one religion.

"After all," she said, "all the monotheistic religions must surely be worshipping the same God, although they may each call their God by a different name. Science, through many different channels, is proving that the 'God-Power' manifested by religious people all over the Earth comes from the same source.

"It is very difficult for the people of Earth to accept a new way of thinking without having a long time to think about it. Man usually tries to alter new concepts to match something he already believes," she continued.

"Since we think of ourselves as 'God's children,' and we know that He teaches us when He feels that we are old enough and experienced enough to know a little more, we can reason that He might possibly feel that we are almost ready to know some things about our Universe that we were not ready to accept two thousand years ago.''

The Acceleration of Time

Several UFO contactees have felt that, for whatever reason, sometime during the year 1965 something ''clicked'' whereby everything advanced. Time accelerated.

Think back to 1965, the contactees will say. Didn't you—and just about everyone you knew—go through a major change at that time? Although it might not have been profoundly evident from a social, economic, or political point of view, things began to happen to people on a very personal level.

Colonel Arthur J. Burks (U.S. Marine Corps, Retired) was a popular lecturer in the field of metaphysics, whose specialty was the exploration of Akashic records of past lives. I was able to ask Colonel Burks about the matter of 1965 shortly before his death.

''This is a peculiar thing, and I think a number of people have taken note of it,'' he said. ''In February and March 1965, I began to get little ideas from people who came in for study. People would come in with the notion that things were moving faster. I came to the conclusion that about February or March 1965 it was as if each person in the world had started to take a step forward, and he or she stepped across a period of years from 1965 to 1995. Since everybody did it, nobody noticed it. And it became evident in the studies I did for people that spirit was taken by surprise.

''After a period of time,'' he went on, ''I found a reading by Edgar Cayce, who said in 1912 that there would be a collapse of time, some interference with time, that would cover a period of years near the end of the century. It seemed to me that these words of Cayce offered some sort of confirmation on this giant move ahead.''

"You're saying, then, that in 1965 everyone took a step into the future?" I asked.

"Everybody stepped across thirty years on the spiritual plane," was his answer. "It is confusing, because in spirit there is no time. I noticed another strange thing. When I made a prediction before 1965, I would be within a couple of days of being right on target. But now I have discovered— and I hear that others have, too—that a prediction will work out all right, but it will be faster than predicted. If I say something will work out in June, it may happen in February. In other words, everything seems to be stepped up.''

According to Dr. Richard L. Rubenstein, Professor of Psychology of Religion, Florida State University in Tallahassee, our extraordinary technological revolution is manifesting itself in shifts in religious attitudes.

"I think society has become far more organized and to a certain extent stratified as a result of the complex kinds of products which society now needs in order to maintain itself," Dr. Rubenstein explained. "I am thinking of jet planes, computers, television cameras and television receiving sets, and the whole realm of services which support such tools. I am also thinking of the vast expansion of the industry of education which has been taking place in the last ten or fifteen years.

"This has required new elements, new ways of apprehending reality as a result of the opportunities made available by the new techniques. Our reality is not the same with a color television set as it was in the world in which one went home in the evening and read by candlelight. Our reality is not the same in a world where almost instantaneously we can be transported to other lands as it was when such trips took thirty days to complete. Furthermore, the complexity of the machine is matched by a complexity in the social organization required to manufacture and distribute these machines. This has changed our lives in an extraordinary number of ways, and as people's lives have changed, as the reality they apprehend is changed, their religious lives are inevitably changed with it,'' Dr. Rubenstein concluded.

The Astral Plane and the Higher Realms

Fred Bell has stated that Semjase told him that the astral plane is a field of energy that exists within the nucleus of the atom and within the particles of the atom itself. Its high energy fields move beyond the speed of light.

Size and space are relative in the astral plane. ''When you are on the astral,'' Fred noted, ''it appears to be a large world—even though it may actually be existing within something very much smaller. The thing to remember is that the energy levels are higher there.''

Semjase has said that the astral plane is created in the universe by the interaction of two or more beings who possess a consciousness of self-awareness (i.e., they are aware of their consciousness and the fact that they have the ability to interact). The astral plane also exists between galaxies.

Whenever a self-aware entity raises its energy field to a certain level, there is created, for example, the velocity of the electron within the nucleus of the atom; and the individual is automatically catapulted into that field. The individual automatically becomes at-one with it.

The Higher Realms begin on the etheric plane, according to Semjase. The beings that exist there are very much like humans, except that the manner in which they clothe themselves is of a simpler nature. The colors on the etheric plane are much brighter than those on Earth, and there is not the distortion of perception that humans often experience.

"The temples on the etheric planes are beautiful," Fred Bell stated. In fact, there is a kind of ashramic vibration throughout the entire plane, indicating that there is more group work going on there. It seems to me that most of the spiritual schools exist on the etheric plane, and they seek to guide help immediately downward to those of us on the physical plane."

Death

"Death is a state of transition between planes," the Space Being OX-HO related through its channel, Robin McPherson. "When an entity has finished a state of being on one plane, he passes to a beginning of another.

"Never fear death. When you begin to breathe the breath of life, you are accepting God's love into your being.

"My dear Earth brothers, can't you see that your short lives are taken up with trivial wants and desires of the flesh? Rise up and be above such matters. Life is the expression of the creative God-spark within each of you. Don't waste time with sadness or malice toward your brother.

"Love, love, live, my brothers, now, right now, for you are alive at this moment and never again will you be able to recapture the essence of this instant in time and space. The Universe is ever-changing, and your evolvement might depend on your action right now.

"If your heart is full of God's light, it will help to illuminate the world. In your being is the magnificence and the grandeur of Creation. Give yourself to God and never fear death."

Cycles of Darkness and of Light

According to Fred Bell, the Pleiadeans are very much aware of the 25,827.5-year cycle that is known as the "Procession of the Equinox." There are 12,000 years of darkness, and then there are 12,000 years of light.

During the 12,000 years of darkness, he explained, the human body's endocrine system cannot respond to a consciousness that is actually available at all times. However, during the 12,000 years of light, the human endocrine system begins to respond to superphysical beingness and consciousness and awareness.

The major cycles are divided into two thousand-plus year cycles which constitute the various zodiacal ages, such as the Age of Aquarius, Pisces, and so forth. And there are smaller cycles, such as those of the seasons and the moon cycles.

About every 2,500 years, during the end of an age, some form of avatar or great spiritual leader appears, Fred said. Not only does the messiah appear, but the mass consciousness of the "acceptance group"—that is, the people who will recognize the avatar's manifestation—are all receptive to the Christ-consciousness. In other words, the entire acceptance group is in the vibration of Christ-consciousness.

The Essenes were a group of teachers who lived during the time of Jesus. They were disciples of the enlightened masters who walked the planet during that era.

"I understand that they were also contactees," Fred commented, "but Semjase has not given me very much information regarding that matter."

Spiritual Evolution

"Man can only reach a state of perfection by growing on all levels of being," declared the Space Being OX-HO to the Light Affiliates. "And man must grow not only in his awareness but in his active doings.

"Perfection is a long time coming to most men. Many lives must be lived in order to attain perfection on even one level. No man is a being of perfection unto himself. Man must gradually find that path which leads him on to further knowledge of his Creator.

"To seek is to perfect oneself.

"Life after life, man stumbles and falls, but gradually, he will come to total awareness and full realization on one thought level. Such a process improves man's soul-being and leads him up the ladder to perfection.

"You have a long, long road ahead of you. You may have many more lives to be lived before you reach that angelic state in which God created you. Don't stray away any longer than possible. You cannot know what magnificence awaits you in the higher realms of being."

The Federation of the Andromeda Council

Fred Bell states that Semjase has defined the Federation of the Andromeda Council as an organization made up of elders from many different planetary and galactic networks. These elders make pacts and agreements in order that a multitude of planetary civilizations might work together.

The Council members are the ones who receive the information from the various exploratory missions. They digest it carefully, then establish the corridors through which the beam ships might travel. In other words, as described by Fred, they regulate travel and police the corridors of space.

The Council also works with the different brotherhoods. Within the Federation they have members who specialize in certain kinds of meditations which allow them to communicate with etheric beings or with entities in other dimensions.

"I have seen many channelings that contactees and psychic-sensitives have received from the Federation," Fred claimed. "It seems to be common for those of the proper telepathic affinity to be able to tune in to this network."

Jesus' Mission to Spaceship Earth

One does not have to spend a great deal of time with the proponents of the Space Age religion before learning that many aspects of the Judeo-Christian tradition have only been updated, not abandoned. Jesus himself, often called "Sananda" by the contactees, has a very important role in the cosmology of the Flying Saucer Movement. But the inclusion of the King of Kings in the Space Beings' theology does not seem to make the orthodox Christian's transition to the new teachings any easier. On the contrary, many of the traditionally devout find it difficult to accept their Lord and Savior as a UFOnaut.

Generally speaking, in the Space Beings' teachings, Jesus of Nazareth is not God but is a *Christ*, an ascended master, who incarnated so that he might demonstrate the Christ-pattern for all humans to achieve in a like manner. Jesus, most extraterrestrials are said to claim, studied with the Essenes during the lifetime which is reported in the Bible. The "lost years" of Jesus are no mystery: Between the ages of twelve and thirty, according to these sources, he was receiving special training aboard a spacecraft or in a remote area of Earth selected by the space entities.

The healing, miracles, and teachings of Jesus are said to have been designed to demonstrate the science of mental power, which is synonymous with God Energy or Creative Energy. Jesus thus transmuted the physical form of objects, including his own body for the resurrection.

When he said that his kingdom was not of the Earth, Jesus is believed to have meant that he had come to tutor Light Workers who would prepare Earthlings for a transition to higher worlds.

The Opening of the Fourth Dimension

Jesus of Nazareth, through the contact Yolanda:

"So many things are developing within the hearts and minds of all men throughout the Earth plane that it is necessary more and more for you to realize how the plans are evolving for the program which you all have come to serve.

"What is happening is that the door between the conscious and superconscious minds is being opened. This we call the opening of the fourth dimension; for the spiritual mind is in the fourth dimension, as you call it.

"As this door opens to the superconscious, which is the mental or idea mind, you will become aware of the purpose not only of your own expression and fulfillment but also the meaning of the universe itself. Others have called this cosmic consciousness. This is a good phrase, for you become aware of the cosmos, you become aware of all the cosmic beings and vibrations of life. . . .

"Therefore, I ask you, and suggest most earnestly and pleadingly, meditate upon this purpose; meditate upon the reason why you are here, why you have come into this life expression at this all-crucial moment for this particular planet.

"Dwell on this, for I tell you we are going into the most important segment of time this planet has known in the last 206,000 years."

Peace

"In all the travail which is about to take place, I never want you people of Earth to forget the star above your heads which is shining radiantly to show you the way to peace," admonished the space intelligence OX-HO through the Light Affiliates. "I know that it will be difficult to realize tranquility in the confusion which will break up communications and shut men off from each other, but remember that you are one, and you will be lifted off the Earth as one.

"Peace is that state of silence in knowing which gives man the strength of his convictions and the knowledge that he is stronger in love. You must have peace of mind, peace of heart and peace of soul, for without these things you will not find contentment in the world. Peace cannot be found under any rock or flower. You must find it yourself.

"Peace is the state of tranquility that the soul knows and feels when it is directed on the path to God.

"The path to God is the most beautiful and real thing that you will ever know. It has such a magnitude of color that you will find yourself in line with each atom and particle in space.

"The world today is desperately searching for peace, and it needs peace for its own salvation. Earth cannot go on fighting the rest of the universe in its completely negative pattern. Earth must link up with the other planets, just as a soul links up with another soul. Join with us, Earth brothers; let us find God together.

"Emanate. Emanate. Emanate the love of God to one another. That is your reason for living. That is the only reason you are here—to give to each other and to create a path directly to the Creator. Lift up the one you pity. Give to the one you dislike. For in doing so, you will change yourself and be all the better for it. Discard the you of the past and bring out the one whom God knows. Most Earth people hide from life.

"If each one of you could truly understand what glory it is to be, to breathe, to look, to understand, to feel, you would never be sad again. Sadness and misery are earthly things. Discard them and show that you are God's by radiating all feelings of love, all feelings of light, all feelings of peace and brotherhood.

"Each man must give up himself before God can completely shine through him."

A Prayer from Outer Space

Ishkomar is an alleged intelligence that claimed to have been recorded into a machine aboard a spaceship thousands of years ago. "Were I to be re-recorded into a human vessel," the entity is said to have told a group in Phoenix, Arizona, that had begun to receive its transmissions, "I would be capable of prayer." By way of illustration, Ishkomar offered the following example:

"My thoughts are now directed to the Father Creator of all that is, ever was, or ever shall be, whose in-going and out-going thought force gives form and being to all that exists in the universe.

"I am, within myself, thankful that I have been created and given the opportunity to live. Within my own being lies the awareness of my individuality, yet also my oneness with all that is, ever was, and ever shall be.

"You have given me a oneness as a sovereign being, and I have created my own kingdom of inner worlds and outer worlds. With responsible attitude, I have accepted my place in time and existence, and by so doing, I have brought peace to my inner worlds and order to my outer worlds.

"My self-appointed task is to bring peace and order to all I may reach in your universe. Not by yoke and forceful domination, but by persuasive reason.

"I cannot judge another sovereign being, but I can help that being to expand its awareness so it may judge itself.

"With honorable purpose, I express my willingness to justify each moment I exist in usefulness to the universal whole, that the universal whole may also justify my existence.

"I stand in a moment of time between the Eternal Past and the Eternal Future, content that, for me, all that was before and all that will be cannot exist for me; and yet I exist because all that was before me gave me my moment in time, and I will share the responsibility for all that will exist in the Eternal Future.

"I recognize the Adversary, the Destroyer, the Deceiver of Worlds—wild, uncontrolled fear that can grow in the intellect of all thinking beings. I know that caution is a progressive thought form from which fear grows. When ungoverned by reason and understanding, it becomes the author of confusion and the enemy of all that is.

"I dedicate my moment in time to the task of bringing peace and order to all beings wherever I may be permitted to touch their intellects with my presence, that in their self-created kingdoms they may establish peace to their own inner worlds and order to their outer worlds by denying fear to exist, thereby committing it to an endless void of eternal disuse.

"Father Creator, your kingdom is mine, for I am aware of it. My kingdom is yours, for because of you, I created it."

13

Chariot/ of God

"**A** messiah is a self-realized being who enters a world to lead the people into enlightenment," Fred Bell said. "Semjase is not any kind of priestess. Semjase and her people are not to be considered as gods. They are just people who are helping. Semjase does not claim to be the Christ or anything like that. She is a follower, just as we are."

A good many contactees are convinced that the Space Beings, in addition to helping us move into the future, offer an exciting blend of science and religion.

A few years ago, the Reverend G. H. Nicholson, rector of the Church of St. Mary the Virgin, Burfield, England, published his views on UFOs in an issue of the church's regular newsletter. The Reverend Nicholson began by discussing the global range of the UFO phenomenon and posed the question of whether these things might be the "chariots of God" mentioned in the Scriptures, or if they might be the instruments of a "Satanically indwelt person on Earth."

The rector next displayed his awareness of the contactees'
basic message: The Space Beings are messengers of God;
their present task is to monitor the Earth and assist in the
Judgment Day that will soon be upon humanity; they will
be responsible for a mass "space-lift" of all of God's true
followers and for the care of these good people on another
world while the Earth is cleansed in a crucible of fire and
destruction.

After cautioning all Christians against the fearful "Satanic Deception" that will seek to delude the entire world
in the last days, and admonishing all good people to test
the Space Beings against the exhortations in Scripture, the
Reverend Nicholson reminded his flock:

> Jesus has shown us that the heavens are inhabited by
> His angels and His elect, and that when He returns, His
> angels will "gather together His elect from the four
> winds and from one end of heaven to the other."
> A prophecy in Psalms tells of the space vehicles in
> this event. "The chariots of God are twenty thousand,
> even thousands of angels; the Lord is among them."

The Reverend Nicholson concluded his affirmation of
belief in the reality of the UFO phenomenon and its possible association with certain of the prophecies in scripture
by saying: "If the saucers should cause us to believe in
God and His word; to repent of our national and individual
sins, and to turn to Him with all of our heart in view of
what surely shall come to pass, they will have served a
very great purpose, in addition to any role they have to
play in the days to come."

Lord Soper, Britain's outspoken Methodist peer, stated
publicly his view that sentient beings could exist in the
universe who have none of the physical sense of man.
"They could exist as a mass of radio waves, or something
equally strange to us who are so used to thinking in
anthropomorphic terms." The clergyman saw no reason to

question one's faith in God if beings from space should ever visit Earth.

"If there is intelligent life on a star like Epsilon Eridani, or on planets circling it, these beings must have their own incarnation of God," Lord Soper said. "This fact should not invalidate at all the picture we have of God in Jesus Christ. Christ is the human photograph of God, but beings on other worlds must have their own appropriate photographs of the Eternal Spirit."

Father Lambert Dolphin, research physicist at California's Stanford Research Institute, has declared: "The mounting evidence leads me to believe that UFOs are extraterrestrial in origin, piloted by intelligent beings. Their appearance in recent years is probably in some way associated with the imminent second coming of Jesus Christ."

Rabbi Norman Lamm, Jewish theologian, issued his opinion that no basic tenet of Judaism would be threatened by the scientific discovery that man is "not the only intelligent and biospiritual resident in God's world."

Although the Bible emphasizes the unique nature of man, Rabbi Lamm points out, such a teaching is not an assertion that the remainder of the universe lacks intelligent life. Such a doctrine simply affirms "the spiritual dignity of creatures endowed with reason and free will."

The Jewish theologian stated that on earth only man fulfills these unique conditions, but "if we should discover other free and rational species, we shall, of course, include them in the community of uniquely biospiritual creatures."

The Reverend Dean Johnson, rector of St. Peter's Episcopal Church, Sycamore, Illinois, and his wife watched an enormous circular UFO descend to nearly treetop level on the shore of Lake Michigan. With Chicago as a backdrop, the Johnsons had the object in view for twenty minutes.

The Reverend Johnson was firm in his statement that the vehicle definitely "was not of this earth." When newsmen quizzed him about the theological implications of visitors from other worlds, the clergyman replied that he had thought "long and hard" about the matter, and said:

> I believe it is possible that just as Christ was the incarnation—or embodiment—of God on Earth, incarnations have appeared to other civilizations in space. But these incarnations could have been different, conceivably in the form of a woman, or even a series of incarnations. For me, the reality of UFOs simply makes me realize that our relationship to God and to the universe is much wider than we have thought.

The Reverend Helmut Wipprech of the United Church of Canada has ventured his opinion that the Biblical descriptions of angels could easily fit "intelligent beings from space." In his view, even the Christmas star of Bethlehem was probably a spaceship, "because stars do not stand still and hover over one place."

The Oneness of Earthlings and Space Intelligences

Semjase has stressed the oneness of Earth people with the Pleiadeans. Fred Bell recalled her words thusly:

"We are all cells in the body of a greater being. If some of the cells are sick, the overall wellness of the being is going to be affected. The frequency or vibration is going to be off for the entire being.

"The Pleiadeans are physical just as we are, and it's important that we are healthy and in fine body and spirit so that the energies and frequencies and signals that we send out to the Universe are also healthy. The Pleiadean consciousness, their scope of beingness, is one that sees the Big Picture, not just the local picture of our solar system. They travel to places like Earth, approach races that aren't quite developed yet—as we are not—and during the proper periods of time (which we are in now where it's permitted) they help develop the awareness to a higher level.

"Realize that all human beings in this present cycle of positive energy, this 12,000-year cycle of light, aren't going to become enlightened. But from this work, 144,000 souls will come, and these 144,000 souls may end up in the Pleiades or in other parts of the galaxy. If some of us evolve to their world, for example, that means a lot.

"They want us to come to their world, but not as entities partially together spiritually. They want us to be at the beginning levels of awareness when we incarnate in their vibratory frequency."

The Space Beings' Age-Old Messages

We Earthlings may be slow learners at this "awareness" task, for it would appear that the Space Beings have been strenuously endeavoring to get us beyond the "beginning levels" for quite some time.

Many readers will be familiar with the New Testament story of Saul, who was struck blind by a brilliant light while on the road to Damascus.

After he had recovered his sight by following instructions given to him in a vision, he changed his name to Paul, became a Christian missionary, and in his epistles to the young churches established a large part of Christian dogma.

Just as Saul was diverted from his journey by a bright light and a period of blindness, the contactee literature tells us of a salesman in South Dakota, a businessman in New Jersey, and a policeman in Nebraska who were temporarily rendered sightless and disoriented by a strange and powerful light, which appeared above them as they traveled along lonely highways.

When these individuals recovered their sight and their

memories, they recalled seeing a spacecraft and an occupant, and receiving a message to share with the world. Although some contactees have remained silent about experiences like these, others have changed their names and their occupations, and have come to devote their lives to preaching of peace, love, brotherhood, and the coming time of transition.

Ezekiel saw a "wheel within a wheel" land before him. Four occupants emerged, and the prophet felt the spirit enter him when one of the beings spoke to him. From that day on, Ezekiel had the gift of prophecy and the ability to work miracles.

Contactee accounts tell of a television copywriter in California, an Air Force pilot in Florida, and a college girl in Washington who observed the landing of unknown aerial vehicles. After communicating with the occupants, who resembled descriptions of traditional angels in that they were fair, golden-haired, and imbued with tranquil assurance, the contactees later discovered that they had remarkable precognitive abilities, the blessing of touch healing, and highly developed clairvoyant abilities.

Moses spoke to the angel of the Lord as it appeared in a pillar of flame near a wilderness bush. The voice from the fire promised Moses divine aid and assistance in performing miracles.

Jacob wrestled with an angel; Abraham fed angels and pleaded with them to spare Sodom and Gomorrah; Joshua received his inspiration to shatter the impregnable walls of Jericho after a confrontation with an angel.

In the last forty years, voices from glowing orbs have spoken to dozens of men and women, who have since forsaken their former callings and have devoted their lives to preparing the Earth for the coming New Age.

And the Space Beings, our "angels in astronaut suits," have begun channeling spiritual guidance to assist humankind to survive both the psychological and physical cataclysms attendant upon the death of an old world and the birth of a new one.

As we have seen throughout this book, the contactees have been told, among other matters, that we are not alone in the solar system, that space intelligences have come to teach us, that we must raise ourselves to higher levels of vibration in preparation for elevation to new dimensions, that we stand on the precipice of a quantum leap forward on both a biological and a spiritual level.

The majority of contactees express a general sense of well-being, a kind of "cosmic consciousness." However, after the initial visitation from a UFOnaut, contactees may experience several days and nights of restlessness. They may have strange dreams of being taken to a crystal city on another planet or in another dimension.

They may attempt to deal with this period of spiritual awakening for several weeks before they find that they can no longer contain the burning fire in their hearts, and they prepare to share with the world their contact with Space Beings. Their commitment is complete and total. Friends and family members closest to the contactees have testified to the fact that they have become literally changed and transformed individuals.

The Space Odyssey Nears Completion

For the UFO contactees it would appear that, in one sense, our space odyssey has come much nearer to completion.

"Semjase has told me that from the lowest being to the highest being, all are perfect in God's imagination," Fred Bell said. "You might switch the word 'perfect' with 'in harmony with the environment and universe.'

"The Pleiadeans with whom I have been in contact are near what I would call perfection in the God-image of a human being. They are more balanced in their spiritual and physical ways of life. They are more 'laid back.' They live longer lifespans. They don't have wars like we do. Their overall group purpose is to help other beings, which you surely can't say about the people of the Earth.

"When you reach out for perfection and realize that you are touching on the Grace of God, you understand that the more evolved races are naturally going to be closer to that evolvement and that expression. I see the Pleiadeans as setting examples that Earth people would want to follow.

"I guess perfection in its final state woud be all things being composed into one entity with that entity achieving perfect harmony with all thoughts, all energies, all forms of creation, and becoming a source of everything. I would say the final aspect of perfection is when the highest source and the lowest grade of pragmatic consciousness become unified in oneness," he concluded.

It is Fred Bell's belief that Space Beings can aid humankind in recognizing its kinship with the Cosmos and its oneness with the universe.

14

A Power Beyond the Ordinary

Moi-Ra and Ra-Ja Dove term themselves "Aquarian Star Shepherds" and consider their Aquarian Perspectives in Lytle Creek, California, to be an interplanetary mission place.

From their point of view, the key word of the Piscean Age was *devotion*, which focused on beliefs as an integral part of life. The key word of the Aquarian Age is *know thyself*, which emphasizes the realization of the godliness in each and every person. The "Star Shepherds" are convinced that there are key concepts that call for the galactic shift that is occurring throughout the omniverse, and with which the Earth is particularly concerned as regards its inhabitants.

In the Piscean Age, Ra-Ja stated, religion was based on a "True Believer's" view in which the adherent, whatever the particular religion he followed, believed in a dominant god and worshipped that god with a zealous faith—even to the extent of killing those who did not "believe" as he did! In all these religions, the focus was on the outside deity rather than a belief in one's innate divinity. Inner divinity was either scorned as anti-god, or of the devil, or as something to work toward or "believe in" but not necessarily put into practice.

Be Still and Know That You Are God

As with so many UFO contactees, Moi-Ra and Ra-Ja Dove are convinced that the Aquarian Age is heralding in a new religion. "Even the word *religion* will not be used anymore," they stated, "for the main crux of the matter will have a much deeper sense of reality. The person will evolve out of *believing in* something and into *becoming* that something. The person will *know*! The individual will know what the religions of the Ancient Age have always tried to demonstrate: to be STILL and KNOW that YOU are GOD!

"Indeed, this is the great new religion! Each and every person will know that he is GOD! The word *religion* will not anymore be applicable in this case, because it originates from the Latin word *religere*, which means reunification with God. At this point in the history of humankind, if beings on the planet Earth realize that they are God, then there is no more need to be reunified with God."

From their "Aquarian Perspective," Ra-Ja explained, you are God with respect to the idea that you are an aspect of God, as the tree, the dog, or the sky all have godly qualities within. If God is omniscient, omnipotent, and omnipresent, then everything is of God and, therefore, *is* GOD!

In the Aquarian Age, so this philosophy asserts, human beings will have evolved out of the archaic need of seeing GOD as existing outside of themselves, and will be free of the burden of having to get down on their knees and worship or pray to some deity in the sky who will scold them if they do not fear Him or offer sacrifices!

Religion, then, which has been primarily defined as a set of rules, dogmas, and beliefs compiled into a system of practices which purport to reunite man with God, will evolve into spirituality. Hence, we need to drop the term *religion* and use the term *spirituality*. With this new galactic-dominant plan, humanity will simply *be*. Not *believe*, but *BE*. Everything we think, feel, and do will be of GOD. No longer will our worship be restricted to some deity whom we have never actually seen, but we will be free to cherish everything, including ourselves!

Humanity will have evolved beyond the need to run to the local priest to find out what GOD has to say for that week. Humanity will be able to look within and *know* what God has to say.

As "religion" will be replaced by "spirituality," according to this Aquarian perspective, "God" will be replaced by "spirit." *God without* will be replaced by *God within* and will be known as the "Spirit" indwelling within all things.

Mediators of Humanity

The adherents of orthodoxy might ask, "But what will happen to my God, to my YHWH, my Jesus, my Krishna, my Mohammed, my Buddha, my Sanat Kumara?" But contactees Moi-Ra and Ra-Ja state that these Great Ones will remain in spirit, as they always have and always will. Yet Earthlings will begin to realize them for what they really are: mediators.

"None of these great Master Souls have really ever proclaimed themselves as the ultimate one GOD!" the Star Shepherds protest. "No! They have always proclaimed themselves as but aspects of the one GOD, just as you are!

Humans will realize themselves as disciples of the Divine Wisdom and will no longer suffer the great karma in the materialistic sense, for they will be free to 'BE.' "

The Return of the Dove

Believing themselves to be entities here on a mission from the "Aquarian Galactic Spirit," Moi-Ra and Ra-Ja Dove feel they have a responsibility to divulge relevant information on the Atlantean cycle and the upcoming galactic plans slated for planet Earth during the Aquarian Age. As have other Light Workers, they have taken up a commitment aeons of time ago to assure the smooth evolution of the planet Earth so that it may once again stand proudly among the other planets in the galaxy as sponsors of omniversal peace and unconditional love!

Ra-Ja has been told that at about the same time that the planet Maldek was destroyed by misuse of energy (nuclear), Atlantis, too, was destroyed by the same misuse of energy. The relevance to this time frame is that humanity is going through the same lessons. But our cosmic and celestial parents, referred to as space people or extra-terrestrials, tell us that humankind will not be completely destroyed by nuclear power, primarily because the Space Beings will not allow it. The planet's human inhabitants still have to learn the proper use of energy.

Moi-Ra and Ra-Ja say they are here living in human bodies to fulfill a galactic mission that they began long ago during the time of Lemuria, Atlantis, Egypt, and Maya. Now in America, this mission, Aquarian Perspectives, will have reached its pinnacle for the Age of Aquarius on a final stage which can be termed "The Return of the Dove" and "The Return of the Plumed Serpent." The teachings of Quetzalcoatl, the Plumed Serpent, will merge with the teachings of the Christ, the Dove.

"Be ye wise as a serpent, yet gentle as a dove." This will be the symbolic representation of the galactic plan now overshadowing mankind.

Ra-Ja has been informed that in the Piscean Age, because of the nuclear problems in the past, the planet Earth had a tear in its atmospheric belt as well as in its own inner world. This caused splits in the astral level of consciousness which caused negative spirits to be created, leading then to deception and destruction. The deception that filtered into religious areas allowed the misconception regarding God and spirituality. The dove was upheld as a universal symbol of love and peace, yet many religious followers, who were supposedly following the Prince of Peace and his dove-like spirit, went about killing native peoples who did not see eye to eye with them.

The powers behind such negativity were the negative laggard thoughts in the astral plane, and the thought forms of confusion that resulted from the misuse of energy. Therefore, politicians and greedy materialists held the helm of religious and government groups rather than the people of Spirit.

Star People, Light Workers, Awaken!

All humans and visiting Star People have a responsibility of invoking the Violet Flame of Transmutation to transform the discord, hate, lust, war, and greed which have enveloped this planet since the original sin of misuse of nuclear energy. All Star People and Light Workers who have taken up the mantle of responsibility to usher in the New Civilization have the prime function of cleansing their beings of all negativities through the use of the Violet Flame, thus prompting the proper transformation that will enable them to perform their mission. Such cleansing will hasten their pace of vibration to synchronize with that of the planet so that all spiritual undertakings may flow with ease.

One only need invoke the Violet Flame and allow the inner eye to see it, and negative energies will be transmuted until they no longer exist in any dimension!

"Return of the Plumed Serpent"

The aim of the Order of the Plumed Serpent is to return to this planet the wisdom that is contained in the appropriate use of technology. We will once again see pyramids of the size and scope of the Great Pyramid in Ghiza, the Temple of the Magicians at Chichén Itzá, and the Temple of Inscriptions at Palenque, as well as of the Great Step Healing Pyramid of Zoser. Spacecraft capable of interstellar flight will dot our skies.

"You must realize that in truth there is only 'goodness' in the Universe," Ra-Ja stated. "All evil or disharmony, by its very nature, is illusion. But the drama has been built up so strongly that only a few—the very brave and the *very pure*—can pierce this illusory veil and know the truth. The Aquarian Age will change all this.

"There is no higher or lower, so the dove is not higher than the serpent. In the very near future, they will become one on this planet."

Corruption in the Earth system has caused political and religious deceit. This is the true cause for the discrepancy in the story of the serpent in the Garden of Eden deceiving wo-man. Actually, nothing could be further from the truth, Ra-Ja and Moi-Ra state, for the extraterrestrial entity that was the serpent was a member of a celestial race who has been working with this planet and who has helped develop the wisdom faculty of humanity. In a similar manner, the Celestial Beings known as "the doves" have helped humanity develop its love nature.

The Aquarian Age will indeed see the intergalactic plan fulfilled on our planet. Hence, the harmonic synchronization of the two natures: the Serpent and the Dove.

"Humankind has been tended in their Garden Planet since the beginning of time by two extraterrestrial races," Ra-Ja commented. "*One*, the Master Avatar Doves or Angels, beneficent beings who bring the higher aspects of love and peace in their wake from many planets, star systems, and even galaxies beyond the Earth. *Two*, the Serpent race, or the wisdom teachers, the technological geniuses.

"The Doves have always taught humanity that the Kingdom of Heaven was within them and that they could realize their own divinity by going within.

"The return of the Plumed Serpent, Quetzalcoatl, will coincide with the return of the Dove, the Christ. Together they will lift humankind out of bondage! Soon, indeed, the lion will lay down with the lamb; and once again, peace and love shall reign throughout the galaxy!" Ra-Ja concluded.

A Spiritual Revolution

In whatever manner the more cautious reader may assess the channeled material in this book, there should be little question remaining that right now thousands of men and women are in the process of creating a spiritual revolution. Throughout this planet, doctors, nurses, college professors, high school teachers, business executives, housewives, truck drivers and common laborers have become regular conduits for messages from entities who allegedly come from other worlds or other dimensions.

The mechanism of channeling communications from such entities permits ordinary people to do extraordinary things. The UFO channelers still look and act pretty much the same as they did before they began communicating with their extraterrestrial guides and teachers, but now they have an edge. They have made contact with a source of power and inspiration beyond the ordinary, and they seem now to utilize increased creative and practical benefits at the forefront of human experience. At the same time, while they have been elevated to higher realms of consciousness and spiritual communion, they have also become one with an eternal and universal brotherhood and sisterhood, a fellowship of beings both seen and unseen.

This innate ability to contact Higher Intelligence is, perhaps, the most important inherited attribute in our birthright as evolving humankind.

In an earlier work *(Medicine Power: The American Indian's Revival of His Spiritual Heritage and Its Relevance for Modern Man*, Doubleday, 1974), I distilled the most essential elements of Medicine, shamanism, into eight spiritual expressions:

1. The vision quest.
2. A reliance on one's personal visions and dreams to provide one's direction on the path of life.
3. A search for personal songs to enable one to attune oneself to the primal sound.
4. A belief in the total partnership with the world of spirits and the ability to make personal contact.
5. The possession of a nonlinear time sense.
6. A receptivity to the evidence that the essence of the Great Mystery may be found in everything.
7. An awareness of one's place in the web of life and one's responsibility toward all plant and animal life.
8. A total commitment to one's beliefs that pervades every aspect of one's life and enables one to walk in balance.

In a metaphysical nutshell, the current interest in channeling guidance from UFO intelligences may be a rediscovery of personal shamanism. Coupled with the awareness that we are all multidimensional beings, the individual shamanic impulse may have been updated by the evolving human psyche to include both the cosmos and our interstellar technology.

Together with hundreds of thousands of men and women throughout our collective species' history, today's channeler of Space Beings is declaring that the nonmaterial self exists within us, that it is capable of being activated as an inner source of inestimable power, and that it is somehow linked to an even greater Source of power and inspiration that permeates and governs the entire universe.

There is nothing of the occult, the satanic, in such a declaration. There is nothing in the innate ability to channel personal guidance that conflicts in any way with organized religion. There is nothing in the manifesting of creative revelation that offends in any way orthodox science.

Sir John Eccles, winner of the 1963 Nobel Prize in Physiology/Medicine for his pioneering work on the communication of nerve cells, openly declared his belief in a nonmaterial and aware "self" that enters our physical brain sometime during embryological development or early childhood. This "ghost in the machine," as Arthur Koestler described it, imbues us with everything that makes us distinctly human: self-awareness, free will, personal identity, creativity, the emotions. What is more, this "ghost" survives after the physical machine dies.

Controlled daydreaming—the process of focusing our unconscious states—may, in the view of Dr. Erik Klinger, "constitute a mental back burner in which information can be organized and reorganized creatively."

Cancer researcher Dr. O. Carl Simonton has achieved marvelous results in directing fantasy projections to bolster the body's immunological system to withstand the ravages of stress, which contributes to so many diseases.

Indeed, when one comes right down to it, such applications of the psyche as channeling Higher Intelligences, fantasy projections, and a sense of wonder may well constitute the central features of the human spirit—and none of us may be able to survive well without them.

Dr. John Lilly, that brilliant researcher into the intelligence of such nonhuman creatures as dolphins and whales, insists that the act of experiencing higher levels of consciousness through altered states, such as those utilized in channeling, is the only way to escape our brain's destructive programming. In other words, channeling may reprogram the brain creatively and positively.

"Flashes of inspiration" have been assessed by psychologist Dr. Eugene d'Aquili as neurological mechanisms which can boost our right brain hemispheres into a separate reality. Cosmic consciousness is triggered when the gestalt right half of the brain convinces the left brain of the validity of the holistic truths which it has perceived.

The kind of cosmic consciousness achieved while men and women are channeling Space Beings may unite them with an energy pattern somewhat akin to Dr. Rupert Sheldrake's morphogenetic field, wherein all living beings may tune in to the experiences—both physical and spiritual—of their predecessors.

Not only does the ability to channel constitute the very basis of creativity, but it also expresses the very essence of individual freedom. Dr. Joseph Campbell has asserted that the spiritual guides for the coming age will be those creative persons who can achieve new types of nontheological revelation for our society. We have clearly seen in this book how UFO channelers are providing an interface of science and religion for hundreds of thousands of today's spiritual seekers.

At the same time, however, it must be recognized that

there are truths that are personal, and there are truths that are universal—and the twain should not be mixed. There are archetypal and symbolical revelations that must be carefully interpreted before they can be disseminated to uncritical audiences.

Truly, there are boundaries that must be observed, and many UFO contactees too readily kick down the fences of reason and run helter-skelter through the dark forest of the unconscious. However, with only modest amounts of self-discipline there are techniques, meditations, and exercises that can be practiced in order to keep the channel pure of personal prejudices and cultural biases.

During the years that I have been interacting with the UFO contactees and their channeled material, I have been intrigued by the number of orthodox clergy who have displayed a genuine openness to the teachings of the Space Brothers. Some clerics find the entire UFO phenomenon offers a kind of timeless physical proof of the mysteries to be found in the Bible. Others feel assured that the Space Beings are really God's angels coming to gather the elect in the ''chariots of God.''

New Age practitioners speak confidently to me of their belief that the UFOs contain spiritual entities who have come to assist struggling humankind in the period of cleansing which must come at the end of the Piscean Age, in preparation for the dawning Age of Aquarius. Once again the ''angels,'' i.e. the space intelligences, are speaking to the prophets, the contactees, in order that we might be guided through the difficult period of transition as a new world rises from the ashes of the old.

And in the considered opinions of a surprising number of orthodox clergy, as well as New Agers, the channeled material that you have read in this book constitutes the new gospels for an evolving religion that will be structured to serve the spirit of the Oneness that will sustain humankind in its space odyssey to the stars.

As in all matters of faith without an abundance of tangible physical evidence, each individual must make his or her own assessment of these gospels for a New Age; for in the final analysis, it is only the individual who must live with the consequences of such a decision.

But if the UFO contactees and their messages of an intergalactic fellowship might enable us to face courageously the ghastly specter of nuclear annihilation . . . to combat unceasingly the sickening ecological horror of what may be an irreversible pollution problem . . . to repent constructively of our national and individual sins . . . to believe steadfastly both in the power of love and in an everlasting Source of strength outside of ourselves, then they shall have served a very great role in helping us to adjust to the days to come. And then, once again, we shall have looked upward to the stars so that we might move onward, into the future, thus continuing the quest for our cosmic birthright.

About the Author

Considered by his peers to be one of the true experts on UFOs, Brad Steiger is the author of one hundred books. He lives in Phoenix, Arizona.